by Andrea Updyke

Klout® For Dummies®

Published by
John Wiley & Sons, Inc.
111 River Street
Hoboken, NJ 07030-5774

www.wiley.com

For general information on our other products and services, please contact our Customer Care Department within the U.S. at 877-762-2974, outside the U.S. at 317-572-3993, or fax 317-572-4002.

For technical support, please visit www.wiley.com/techsupport.

Wiley publishes in a variety of print and electronic formats and by print-on-demand. Some material included with standard print versions of this book may not be included in e-books or in print-on-demand. If this book refers to media such as a CD or DVD that is not included in the version you purchased, you may download this material at http://booksupport.wiley.com. For more information about Wiley products, visit www.wiley.com.

Library of Congress Control Number: 2013935677

ISBN 978-1-118-50537-3 (pbk); ISBN 978-1-118-50544-1 (ebk); ISBN 978-1-118-50550-2 (ebk); ISBN 978-1-118-51482-5 (ebk)

Manufactured in the United States of America

10 9 8 7 6 5 4 3 2 1

About the Author

Andrea Updyke is the Founder of Lil-Kid-Things (www.lilkidthings. com), a parenting blog that focuses on raising boys, thriving as a work-at-home mom, and facing the challenges of parenthood head-on. She is a freelance writer and social media junkie.

Andrea has been connecting with people online since 1993 and had her first website in 1998. Her first blog was born in 2003, and she has been on Facebook since 2004 and an active Klout member since 2010. She has a Klout Score of 66.

Dedication

This book is dedicated to my husband, Gerald Updyke, for his support and loving encouragement throughout the entire writing process and to my sweet boys, Oscar and Calvin, who completed my life the moment I laid eyes on them. Dream big, boys. Anything is possible.

Author's Acknowledgments

I would like to thank my friends and family, both online and offline, who have supported me with notes of encouragement, texts, questions, and cheers as I reached each deadline. Knowing I had a team of support behind me kept me moving forward and excited to see this project through to its completion. Thank you to my editors on the *For Dummies* team, who so patiently guided me and answered my questions, and to Starbucks for being my home away from home on marathon writing days. Finally, I want to thank my amazing mom, Doreen Lawrence, for sacrificing so many of her days to watch my boys so that I could write. To both of my parents, thank you for believing in me and for always cheering the loudest.

Publisher's Acknowledgments

We're proud of this book; please send us your comments at http://dummies.custhelp. com. For other comments, please contact our Customer Care Department within the U.S. at 877-762-2974, outside the U.S. at 317-572-3993, or fax 317-572-4002.

Some of the people who helped bring this book to market include the following:

Acquisitions and Editorial

Project Editor: Heidi Unger

Acquisitions Editor: Amy Fandrei

Copy Editor: Amanda Graham

Technical Editor: Michelle Krasniak

Editorial Manager: Kevin Kirschner

Editorial Assistant: Anne Sullivan

Sr. Editorial Assistant: Cherie Case

Cover Photo: © Duncan Walker / iStockphoto

Composition Services

Project Coordinator: Patrick Redmond

Layout and Graphics: Melanee Habig

Proofreader: Melissa Cossell

Indexer: Potomac Indexing, LLC

Publishing and Editorial for Technology Dummies

 Richard Swadley, Vice President and Executive Group Publisher

 Andy Cummings, Vice President and Publisher

 Mary Bednarek, Executive Acquisitions Director

 Mary C. Corder, Editorial Director

Publishing for Consumer Dummies

 Kathleen Nebenhaus, Vice President and Executive Publisher

Composition Services

 Debbie Stailey, Director of Composition Services

Contents at a Glance

Table of Contents

Introduction

If you're a regular Internet user, chances are you participate in one or more social networking sites like Facebook, Twitter, or Google+. Perhaps you use these sites for business or for recreation or a mixture of both. Whatever your intention, the fact is, everything you say is an extension of you and/or your brand, and the influence you build can either help or hinder your online reputation.

Have you ever wondered if the words you put out into the universe via the Internet are influencing anyone? The creators of Klout.com believe they are, and not just that — they believe they've developed a tool that can measure that influence and provide you with insights that may help you increase the power of your online voice. If you're looking to maximize the effects of your online influence, *Klout For Dummies* is a valuable tool to help you accomplish your goals.

Klout is a measurement tool for social media influence. But it's more than an analytics program. In fact, I like to think of it as supplemental to traditional measures of analytics because Klout doesn't simply measure traffic, but actual engagement from individuals you interact with across your various social networks like Facebook and Twitter.

Through Klout, you can measure your online influence, claim fun Perks, participate in philanthropic programs, and endorse other influencers for their talents. It's a mixture between fun and function in which you can group together influencers in certain topics or brands that you want to connect with. Use the +K feature to endorse your colleagues and boost their influence in the process.

Klout believes that everyone has influence, from a prominent blogger or a small businessperson to a student who likes to share his or her taste in music. Klout created this measurement to allow people to understand that influence and learn how to maximize their online voices. The Klout algorithm is not a perfect measure of influence, of course. But as the folks at Klout continue to update it, they improve its accuracy for every influencer.

About This Book

Klout For Dummies is designed to help you achieve your goals using Klout, whether that includes learning what the service is all about or how to make the most of your Klout Score.

You can use this service recreationally or to grow your business. Whatever your motivation, the tools provided in this book arm you with the information you need to create your account and monitor the growth of your online influence. You learn to read the stats in your Klout Dashboard and drill down to get more information about what status updates inspire the most action and create the most engagement. Follow the instructions to take Klout with you by downloading the app on your mobile device, and donate your influence to pay it forward by participating in Klout for Good initiatives.

You don't have to read the chapters in order (though you can). Likewise, don't expect to memorize every process. Refer to this guide as often as you need for some clarification or direction on a particular topic. You should dive in wherever you feel comfortable to get the information you need so you can get back online and start influencing!

How This Book Is Organized

This book is organized using chapters that explain everything from connecting to Klout using Twitter or Facebook to finding other influencers and claiming Klout Perks. You also learn about privacy settings and how to control what appears on Klout when people search for you.

You can read the book from cover to cover or simply thumb through to the section that meets your needs.

If you're new to Klout, I suggest starting with Chapter 1 to read about what Klout is and what it isn't. Then go through the book based on your personal interests. If you have any questions, use the index in the back of the book to search for specific terms quickly.

Foolish Assumptions

When writing this book, I had a new user in mind. I'm assuming that you don't have a lot of prior experience using Klout or its services and therefore I take much of the space in this book explaining the basics of the website and how to use it.

I also assume that you're interested in using Klout to maximize your online influence or at the very least, to understand how you are influential in the online space. I make references to blogging or business and although you can certainly use Klout recreationally, I write with the basic assumption that you have something to gain from increasing your online influence in the social media space.

When I mention using your browser or other social media networks like Facebook and Twitter, I assume that you're familiar with these processes. I don't go into great detail when it comes to social networks except to explain how they connect to Klout. Likewise, I assume that you know how to use your computer and/or mobile device apart from the instructions I give regarding Klout.

Whether you're using this book to learn about Klout, learn how to get Perks, use Klout as a brand, or simply grow your influence, this book helps you achieve your goals.

Icons Used in This Book

I use icons occasionally to draw your attention to information that you may need at a glance. Below are the icons you might see in this book.

When you see the Tip icon, I'm giving you special information about using Klout that may not be obvious when using the site. Read these tips in the context of the instructions presented with them to get the whole picture.

I use the Remember icon to recall useful information that I've previously discussed in another section. Concepts in Klout often overlap, so I tie them together when appropriate to simplify the service as much as possible.

Technical stuff is an icon that I use to call your attention to more detailed information. This may pertain to technical information that may be useful to the more experienced Internet user.

The Warning icon is a quick reminder to proceed with caution when making a specific action or choice within Klout or the Klout mobile app that may be difficult to undo.

Where to Go from Here

Remember to have fun with this book and with Klout. It can be easy to get mired down in social media metrics and technical information, but at the heart of it all is the very definition of social media; that is, using media to be social. It's fun to watch your Klout Score rise, but remember that it's just one of many ways to measure social influence.

I am always available to help if you get stuck on a certain process or concept. Feel free to connect with me anytime on the *Klout For Dummies* Facebook Page located at www.facebook.com/klout fordummies, on Klout at http://klout.com/#/andreaupdyke, or on Twitter at http://twitter.com/andreaupdyke.

Occasionally, we have updates to our technology books. If this book does have technical updates, they'll be posted at www.dummies.com/go/kloutfdupdates.

Chapter 1

Discovering Your Klout

● ●

● ●

*K*lout is an online service that measures your social influence. The creators behind the website believe that every individual has some influence in the online world and their goal is to help you maximize that influence.

But measuring your influence isn't the only thing you can do with Klout. By observing trends in your online usage with the Klout tools, you can see what your community connects with and how others respond to your status updates, and you can identify areas where your conversations can improve and spark more engagement from your followers.

Calculating Your Influence in Social Networks

Klout uses more than 400 variables to measure your Klout Score. Many of them come from networks you probably use every day, such as Facebook, Twitter, Google+, foursquare, LinkedIn, Klout, and most recently Wikipedia. The following sections give you the basics on how Klout measures your online social influence.

Defining Klout

According to Klout, the definition of *influence* is "the ability to drive action." When you build your online community and use it to advance your personal and business goals, you naturally become more influential and thus inspire more people to action based on your topics of influence, information you share, and connections you make online. The more actions you inspire, the greater your influence.

What seems like a very simple service is actually quite complex. Using an algorithm that pulls data from hundreds of variables, Klout assigns scores between 1 and 100 (as shown in Figure 1-1, my Klout Score is 64) to every online influencer based on engagement within his or her social networks (such as Facebook or Twitter).

Klout Score

Figure 1-1: Your Klout Score measures your online influence.

Klout has revised its algorithm several times, each time claiming more detail and therefore, more accuracy for your score. As with many online measurement tools, their work is never done. Klout continues to correct, revise, and improve its service with each new update they make to their algorithm.

Identifying actions and engagement that contribute to your Klout Score

Anytime you connect a social network to Klout (which I tell you how to do in Chapter 7), the service immediately begins measuring

your influence by observing the engagement or actions you generate. Actions can include any of the following:

✔ **Mentions:** Using sites like Facebook, Twitter, and Google+,
Klout evaluates the number of mentions you receive (as
shown in Figure 1-2) and factors that into your overall score.
In social media, a *mention* is when someone tags you by
name within a social network, connecting the update to you.
Typically, you can tag someone by putting the @ symbol
before his or her name or username. The more people mention your name on these networks, the higher level of engagement you have than someone with fewer mentions.

Figure 1-2: Mentions on Google+ influence your Klout Score.

✔ **Likes:** Typically, Likes (on Facebook) or +1s (on Google+) tell
Klout that people see your updates and are reacting to them
in a positive way. When a social media friend sees your post
and clicks Like or +1, friends in her community who may not
yet follow you can see this activity and potentially be influenced as well. Remember that your personal privacy settings
within each network will determine who sees this activity.

✔ **Shares, retweets, and tips:** Even more exciting than a Like for
an online influencer is a Share (on Facebook and Google+) or
a retweet (on Twitter). When you post content and a friend

passes that content on to her friends or followers with a Share or retweet (see Figure 1-3), your influence reaches an entirely new community.

Your influence also gets a boost when someone completes one of your tips on foursquare, such as trying out a restaurant you suggested through the app.

Retweet notification

Figure 1-3: You can see that one follower retweeted this tweet.

✔ **Comments or Timeline posts:** Comments on any post in your connected networks only improve your Klout Score. Likewise, when a person comes directly to your Facebook or Google+ profile and leaves a comment, Klout views this as positive behavior based on your influence.

✔ **Follower and subscriber count:** The number of friends, followers, and subscribers to your social media accounts matter, but they don't matter much. Klout does take into consideration your follower and subscriber count on networks such as Facebook, Twitter, and Google+. However, Klout's philosophy is that engagement trumps numbers every time.

✔ **Links in:** With the addition of Wikipedia as a measurement in Klout's algorithm, real-world influence is now a part of the equation. This means that information on your Wikipedia page may factor into your score, including links in from other websites.

✔ **+K:** You can give and receive +K within Klout itself, as shown in Figure 1-4. The number of +K you receive from others (described in Chapter 7) increases your score by a limited amount within a 90-day period. Klout sets this cap to discourage people from trying to game the system and artificially inflate their scores.

Give +K

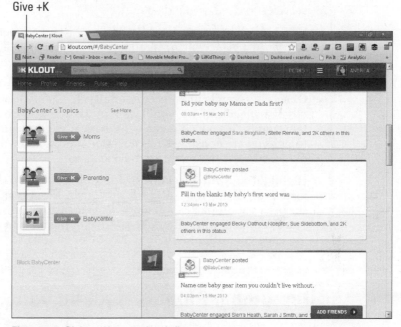

Figure 1-4: Giving +K to another influencer.

Klout is continually including new social networks in their algorithm. Connecting your networks to Klout is the best way to find your most accurate score of influence. It's a fun way to see how you connect with people online and a great tool for evaluating which topics and types of information generate the most engagement. For more information about how to connect additional networks to your Klout account, see Chapter 7.

Benefiting from Klout

Overall, Klout's goal is to help you recognize and harness the power of your own influence whether you affect 10 people or

10,000. Here I identify the specific tools and techniques in Klout that you can use to accomplish that — and as a bonus, earn free merchandise along the way.

You can find several ways to benefit from using the free service, including the following:

- **Enjoying Klout Perks:** Perks are awarded to influencers based on Klout Score, location, and topics of influence as discussed in Chapter 8. Perks are a great way to try new products and services for free or at a discount.

- **Measuring engagement:** By viewing your Klout Moments, you can see at a glance the posts that garnered the most attention in your social media networks. You can also see which networks are stronger for you in terms of responses to your posts.

- **Observing trends in your community:** If you are looking to target a specific niche, you'll want to use Klout to observe certain trends. See which posts get the most engagement, what topics you are considered to be influential in, and what other influencers in your niche are talking about.

- **Highlighting your specialties with topics:** As you use social media to discuss your interests and goals, Klout recognizes these as your topics of influence. This measurement allows you to connect with other like-minded individuals as well as matches you with brands that may be of interest to you.

Deciding if Klout is right for you

Social media experts are divided when it comes to Klout, so it's a good idea to take a few minutes to decide if you even want to participate in the social scoring site.

One school of thought is that Klout still has a long way to go in perfecting the algorithm so it provides a true measure of online influence. Complaints include impossibly high Scores for some people and improbably low Scores for obvious experts in their field. Some people are not comfortable with the idea of a Score in the first place and have decided to opt out completely.

It's true that some marketers and public relations firms are taking Klout Scores into consideration, but the jury is still out on how much weight they put on an influencer's Score. In my experience, an influencer's Klout Score is just one of many different measurement tools — a very small piece of the puzzle.

Still, many people enjoy seeing what happens to their Score and which online activities make a difference. Klout Perks are also a draw, and as long as companies are willing to offer them, the influencers will continue to claim them. Your participation is entirely voluntary.

Observing trends in your niche by using the Search feature

You might want to target a specific group of people from time to time based on a certain topic of influence. Doing so helps you grow your community and potentially make new connections. Klout can help you observe key influencers and display their latest topics of discussion when you use Klout's Search tool.

For instance, if you want to reach people using the Klout topic of moms, enter the word *moms* into the search bar at the top of any page on Klout as pictured in Figure 1-5.

Figure 1-5: Use the search bar to find influencers and discussions.

After Klout finds the search term, you have the following options in the page that opens. You may view information based on influencers or top moments.

✔ **Influencers:** At the top of the screen is a list of influencers (as shown in Figure 1-6) who have the word *moms* in their username or as one of their topics of influence. From here you may click an Influencer's name to view her profile or click the link that says See All Influencers to reveal even more choices.

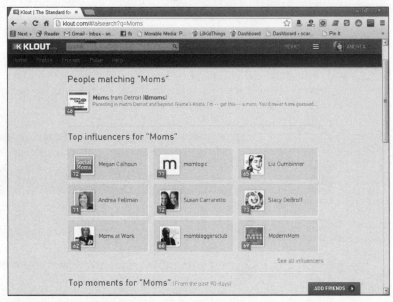

Figure 1-6: A list of influencers appears when I search for the word *moms.*

✔ **Top Moments:** Below the listed Influencers, you can view a list of top moments related to the topic you typed into the search bar. Ten moments are shown by default (shown in Figure 1-7), but you can select Show More at the bottom of the page to increase the number of results.

Following trends is a fun way to grow your community and join the conversation with like-minded individuals. The Search feature within Klout continues to get more sophisticated with each update.

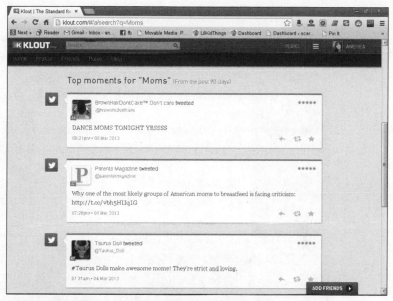

Figure 1-7: Top Moments related to the topic of moms.

Connecting with your audience

After you have identified some of the key trends in your community, you can use that information to connect with your audience in a deeper way. Even if you are a blogger operating as a brand and using social media, you connect with your followers on an individual, organic level.

You can use Klout to identify key interests and learn more about which topics drive the most actions from your followers. Knowing what your community loves talking about increases your ability to create quality conversations and keep them going.

For instance, I can look at my Klout Dashboard (discussed in more detail in Chapter 3) at a glance and see in the highlights from the past 90 days that most of my connections were made via Facebook and Twitter. Klout even takes it one step further by rating each moment from one to five dots (with five being the strongest) to signify the strength of my post's engagement, as shown in Figure 1-8.

Engagement rating

Figure 1-8: A post with strong engagement in my community.

To increase engagement within your social networks, check in with your Klout Dashboard on a regular basis. Doing so is a great way to get a snapshot of the actions you inspire within your community. You can then learn from this information and use it to improve the quality of your social media posts.

Chapter 2

Creating Your Klout Account

*B*efore you can take advantage of everything Klout has to offer, you must set up your user account and profile, and this chapter helps you do just that. Joining Klout is easy because you create your account simply by connecting through one of your existing social networks like Facebook or Twitter.

When you're setting up your account, you can connect other social networks that you use, such as Google+, Instagram, and LinkedIn. Or you can connect them later, and I tell you how to do that in Chapter 7. Theoretically, the more accounts you connect to Klout, the more accurately Klout can measure your influence (which is also called your Klout Score).

You can also configure your e-mail settings, choose a bio to display, and set your profile picture. Once you have your information stored, you can view your public profile, which is the screen that other Influencers will see when they search for you on Klout.

Joining Klout

To join Klout, you first need to sign in to either your Facebook or Twitter account. Doing so ensures that you can connect via one of these networks to create your Klout account. When you sign in to your Klout account in the future, you will do so by connecting via Facebook or Twitter rather than entering a username and password that's unique to Klout. (See Figure 2-1.)

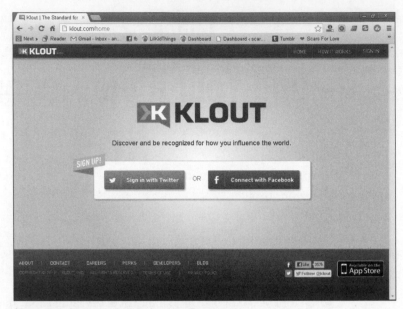

Figure 2-1: Connect via Facebook or Twitter.

To create your new Klout account, follow these steps:

1. **Point your browser to** www.klout.com.

2. **Click Sign In in the upper-right corner of the screen or choose between the Connect via Twitter or Facebook buttons in the middle of the screen.**

3. **Select the social network you want to use to complete your sign-in (either Twitter or Facebook).**

   If this is your first time logging into Klout, you will need to authorize the site to connect to the social network you chose via an authorization page that appears. You will need to be signed in to the Twitter or Facebook account you wish to use in order to continue.

   • *If you sign in with Twitter, you need to allow the Klout application to access your Twitter information as noted in Figure 2-2. Click Allow.*

   • *To connect via Facebook, you need to allow the application to access your Facebook information. Click Go to App and then Allow.*

   A new screen appears on the Klout web page shown in Figure 2-3.

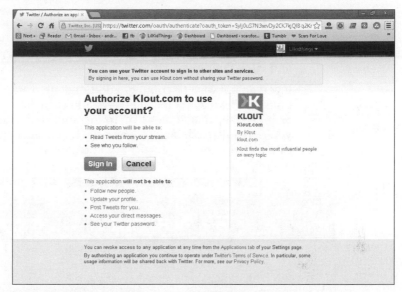

Figure 2-2: Authorize Klout via your existing Twitter account.

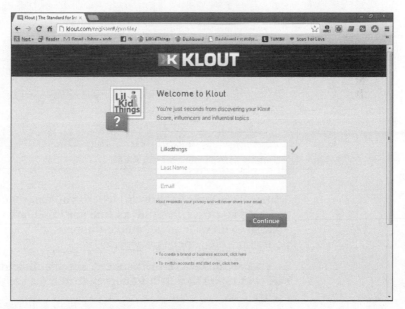

Figure 2-3: Enter your user information.

4. **To create an individual account, your first and last name will populate from your connected social network. You will enter your e-mail address here as well.**

5. **Click Continue.**

6. **To connect more networks to Klout at this time, use the slider buttons on the screen that appears (in Figure 2-4) and click Continue.**

If you do not wish to connect additional networks at this time, don't worry! You can always add them later. Click the Skip this Step link to move on to the next step. Later, when you're ready to connect more social media accounts to Klout, check out Chapter 7 for instructions.

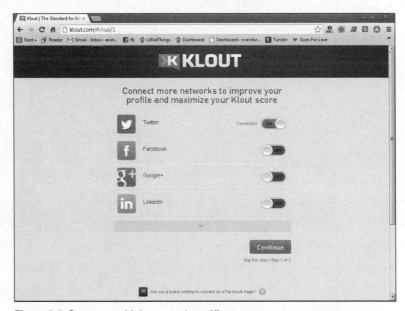

Figure 2-4: Connect multiple networks to Klout.

You now see your Dashboard where you can select topics in which you are influential as well as people who influence you based on your social media interactions (on any of your connected social networks).

7. **To choose topics and influencers, simply click any of the relevant topics and influencers pictured (as shown in Figure 2-5).**

Your account is now active and you are directed to your profile. Here you are able to monitor your Klout Score and make changes to your account in the future.

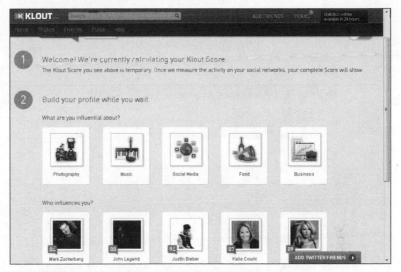

Figure 2-5: Choose from a list of topics and influencers.

After you sign up, you can begin to customize your profile and your communication settings.

Setting Up Your Profile

Klout is only as good as the information you provide, so be sure to fill out your profile with as much detail as you're comfortable sharing. Doing so allows Klout to offer the best user experience possible whether you use the website as an individual or on behalf of a brand.

Klout asks for basic details such as your name and e-mail address, input on how you'll allow Klout to interact with your Facebook account, and your mailing address so that the company can send prizes to you.

When you log in to Klout (by signing in via Twitter or Facebook) you see your name in the upper-right corner of the screen. Select your name and choose Settings from the drop-down menu that appears (as shown in Figure 2-6).

Settings

Figure 2-6: Navigate to your Settings page.

Using Klout as an individual influencer or as a brand

Your first option (at the top of the Profile Settings page) is to choose whether you plan to use Klout as an individual influencer or as a brand influencer. Both options are eligible for Perks, so it's up to you to decide how you want to use this section. Even though I am a blogger and consider my blog a brand, I am known online by my real name and therefore use Klout as an individual. This chapter focuses on using Klout as an individual, but you can check out Chapter 13 to learn more about using it as a brand.

If the I Am an Individual Influencer radio button is selected, the page looks like Figure 2-7. (If instead you choose to participate as a brand, the interface asks for the brand name and eliminates the Gender and Birthday fields.)

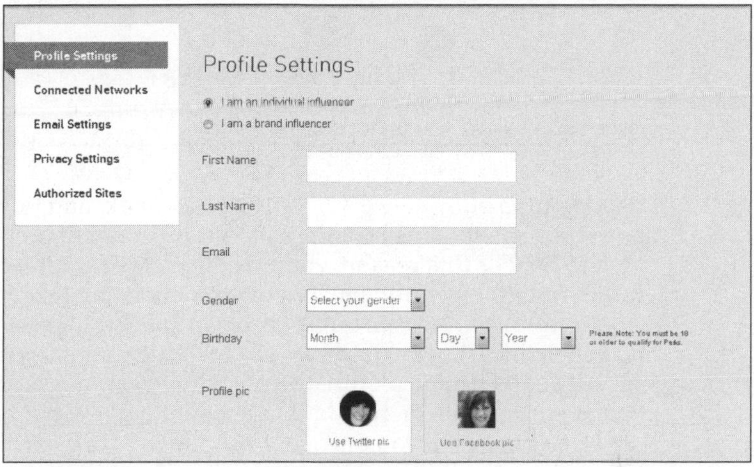

Profile Settings

- Profile Settings
- Connected Networks
- Email Settings
- Privacy Settings
- Authorized Sites

Profile Settings

◉ I am an individual influencer
○ I am a brand influencer

First Name

Last Name

Email

Gender   Select your gender ▾

Birthday   Month ▾   Day ▾   Year ▾   Please Note: You must be 18 or older to qualify for Perks.

Profile pic

Use Twitter pic   Use Facebook pic

Figure 2-7: Klout Profile Settings page.

Complete the following fields with your personal information:

- ✔ **First name (or brand name, if you've chosen to participate as a brand)**
- ✔ **Last name**
- ✔ **E-mail address you wish to use to receive e-mails from Klout**
- ✔ **Your gender (optional; not requested if you're participating as a brand)**
- ✔ **Your birthday (required to verify eligibility for Perks for which you must be 18 years or older; not requested if you're participating as a brand)**

All of the above information is required to use Klout with the exception of disclosing your gender, which is voluntary.

Certain brands may choose to factor gender into their eligibility criteria for Perks, so keep that in mind when deciding whether or not to disclose your gender.

Choosing your profile picture

Your next task is to choose the profile picture you want to associate with your Klout account. You have two options as shown in Figure 2-8.

Figure 2-8: Choosing your profile picture.

Called your *identity networks,* Twitter, Facebook, and Google+ are the three networks Klout uses to verify that you are who you claim to be. For this reason, your profile picture is directly integrated from the identity network of your choosing (except for Google+ at this time). Currently, you can choose between Twitter and Facebook. Choose the account you prefer, and Klout adds that account's profile picture to your Klout account. Anytime you change your profile picture in that account, your Klout profile picture also changes. If you only connect one network to Klout, your profile picture will automatically populate from that account.

Creating your bio

Next is the About section, or your bio. You can opt to use your Twitter description here or you can select the Use this Instead radio button to supply your own information in the text box (see Figure 2-9). This is a great place to share a few of your interests, what you are reading, or even where you blog. This allows people who view your profile to learn a little bit more about you.

Figure 2-9: Tell Klout a little bit about yourself.

Allowing Facebook permissions

Below your bio information, you have the option to allow certain permissions to Facebook. Three different options are shown (see Figure 2-10).

> ✓ **Timeline updates:** Klout gives you the option to allow updates to your Timeline when you earn achievements or give +K (discussed in Chapter 7) to your friends. If you wish to allow this feature, select the Add Klout to Your Facebook Timeline check box. This is voluntary and not required to use Klout.

✔ **See Page Likes:** You have the option to allow Klout to see the Pages you like on Facebook, which is also voluntary. In doing so, Klout may use the information to connect you with Perks or other information that may interest you based on your Facebook Page Likes. To allow Klout to access this information, select the Allow Klout to See Which Pages You Like on Facebook check box in the Facebook section of your Klout Profile Settings page.

✔ **See Friend Lists:** You can also allow Klout to view any Friend lists you have created on Facebook. To allow Klout to access this information, select the Allow Klout to Read Your Friend Lists check box.

Each time you select one of these check boxes, a Facebook permissions dialog box appears. Finalize your permission by selecting Allow in this dialog box.

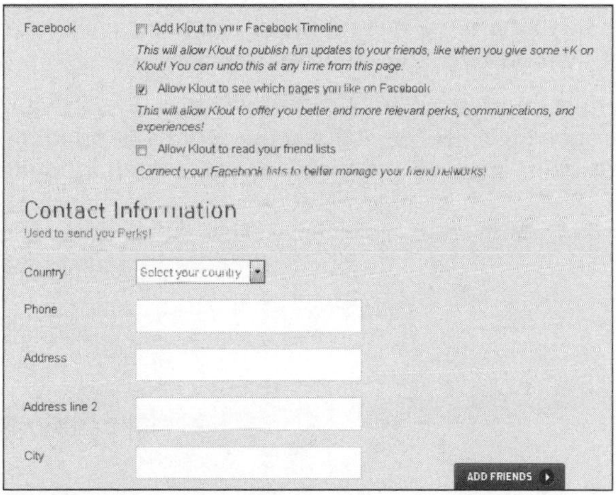

Figure 2-10: Facebook permissions.

Providing contact information

The final step in completing your profile is to enter your mailing address. Klout does not post your address in your public profile, but it does use it to ship your claimed Perks to your home. However, if you do not wish to save this information in your profile, you can still claim Perks, and Klout asks you to provide it at that time (see Chapter 8 for more info on Perks).

When you are finished updating your profile, click the Save Settings button at the bottom of the page and you're finished!

Configuring your e-mail settings

Now that you are officially recognized as an influencer in Klout, select the number and frequency of e-mails you receive from Klout such as notifications of new Perks and when another influencer gives you +K.

To tell Klout how often you'd like to receive e-mail notifications and indicate whether you'd like to receive e-mail updates about Klout, hover the mouse over your name in the top-right corner of the page and select Settings from the drop-down menu. Choose Email settings (shown in Figure 2-11) from the list on the left of your screen and make your choices according to the following options:

- ✔ **Daily digest:** Select this option to get an e-mail daily, at most, with your notifications from the site.

- ✔ **Weekly summary:** Select this check box to get your e-mailed notifications weekly rather than daily.

- ✔ **General updates:** Select this check box if you're interested in receiving weekly e-mails about what's happening on Klout. These updates are not specific to you as an influencer.

Figure 2-11: Email Settings page.

You can provide a different e-mail address if you prefer not to receive e-mails at the address you provided on your profile page.

Klout also offers a series of options (Figure 2-12) for e-mails pertaining to Perks. These e-mails are sent daily.

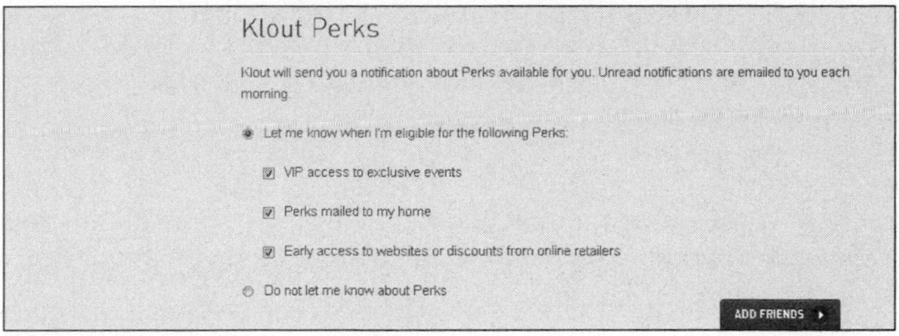

Klout Perks

Klout will send you a notification about Perks available for you. Unread notifications are emailed to you each morning.

⦿ Let me know when I'm eligible for the following Perks:

☑ VIP access to exclusive events

☑ Perks mailed to my home

☑ Early access to websites or discounts from online retailers

○ Do not let me know about Perks

ADD FRIENDS ▶

Figure 2-12: Klout Perks e-mail options.

You may choose between the following:

✔ **Select the Let Me Know When I'm Eligible for the Following Perks option** to choose which e-mails you would like to receive. Then select one or all of the choices below:

- *VIP access to exclusive events:* By selecting this option, Klout sends e-mails to you whenever Perks include VIP access to events near you.

- *Perks mailed to my home:* Selecting this check box allows Klout to send you an e-mail anytime a Perk you've claimed is sent to your home or when you're eligible for a new Perk.

- *Early access to websites or discounts from online retailers:* If you want to receive e-mail notification when you're eligible for early access to new website services or online discounts, select this check box.

✔ **Select the Do Not Let Me Know about Perks option** if you don't wish to receive any e-mails pertaining to available Perks.

Click the orange Save Settings button to save your e-mail preferences.

Viewing Your Public Profile

After you've saved your profile settings, take a look at what everyone else will see when they look at your Klout page! You can check out your page by selecting Profile from the navigation bar at the top of your screen.

On your profile page, you see your profile picture and bio in the upper-left corner along with any networks you have connected to Klout. Your highlighted moments (as discussed in Chapter 3) are shown on the right of the screen. This is the public profile that any person or brand sees when they click on your account.

Within your Klout account, you can see some details regarding how your Klout Score is calculated. I tell you about that in the next chapter.

Chapter 3

Examining Your Klout Dashboard

In This Chapter

▶ Using Klout terminology

▶ Decoding your Klout Score

▶ Highlighting influential Moments

*Y*our Klout Dashboard acts as a starting point each time you log in to your account. A range of options on your Dashboard measure your social media activity, which posts are the most popular, and how you inspire engagement from others via your social media accounts (such as Facebook and Twitter). You can view statistical information about how your Klout Score has changed over time, and see which social interactions were the most influential via Klout Moments and which social networks provide you with the most engagement from your followers.

Learning the Language of Klout

As you navigate your new Klout Dashboard, you may notice a few terms that require a bit of definition. To start, Klout itself is a play on words for the English word *clout,* which means a pull or strong influence, and the concept of online influence is at the heart of your Klout Score. The minds behind Klout believe that everyone has influence and they're constantly updating the algorithm to be as accurate as possible.

Your influence is your ability to inspire online actions in response to your posts. The more engagement or conversation you have within your networks, the more influence you are perceived to have.

Your Klout Score rates your online influence on a scale of 1 to 100. The purpose of the score is to have an at-a-glance metric for brands and influencers to understand how influential someone may be online. Of course, your Score depends on your willingness to use Klout and connect your networks to the service. If you choose not to do this, your Score may not be as accurate.

Klout Moments are a collection of posts from all of your connected networks that garnered the most engagement. You may view your Moments via your Klout profile page or your Dashboard.

Interpreting Your Klout Score

The essence of Klout is the Klout Score, which is a measure of your online influence. When you connect a network such as Twitter, Facebook, or Google+ to Klout, your interactions are immediately included in the hundreds of datum used to determine online influence. The higher your Score, the more online influence you have.

One of the great things about Klout is that you can easily access feedback and analysis regarding your online influence, which can help you decide what actions to take to increase your influence and your Klout Score. The service also makes it easy to compare your Score with that of other influential people and share your Score with your social network.

Finding your Klout Score and Dashboard

When you log in to Klout, the default home page is your Dashboard. An orange speech bubble with a number in it is shown in the top-left side of the screen, next to your name and avatar as shown in Figure 3-1. This number is your current Klout Score.

Klout updates Scores on a daily basis, so some fluctuation from day to day is considered normal.

To learn more about your Klout Score, navigate to your Dashboard by clicking the Home button in the upper-left corner of the screen. This is your Dashboard, which shows your Score, name, and connected networks at the top of the page and highlights your most engaging social interactions on the rest of the page.

To see details regarding your Klout Score, click the Show Stats On/Off button on the right side of your Dashboard (shown in Figure 3-2). A stats section appears within the page.

Home

Klout Score

Figure 3-1: Find your Klout Score in the orange speech bubble.

Figure 3-2: The Klout Dashboard.

Reviewing your Score stats

The Stats section provides lots of great details about your Klout Score, as you can see in Figure 3-3. You can turn the Stats section on and off using the slider in the upper-right corner of your Dashboard.

Figure 3-3: Stats within my dashboard.

Within your stats, you can analyze your Klout Score a variety of ways.

> ✓ **Score history:** Your 90-Day Score History (shown in Figure 3-4) is an interactive graph that shows your score's growth. Hover over this graph, and a pop-up slider appears with the date and your Klout Score for each of the 90 days. As the graph moves up or down, you can see your Score's growth trend and how much your Score really fluctuates.

Figure 3-4: A 90-day Score history on the Klout Dashboard.

To the left of your 90-Day Score History is the percentage your Score has changed in the past day. Although your Score reports in whole numbers, often the change is actually only a fraction of a point.

✔ **Contributions:** To the right of the overview of your Score history, you see another chart that displays the percentage of your Klout Score that comes from each of your social networks. The network with the highest Score is displayed in the middle of the chart. My influence comes primarily from Facebook (52%), as shown in Figure 3-5. You can use the mouse pointer to hover over the chart to see how much each network contributes to your Klout Score. When I hover over my chart, it shows the following contributions: Twitter (40%), LinkedIn (3%), Klout (3%), and Google+ (2%).

Figure 3-5: Klout Score Contributions.

✔ **Connected networks:** To the right of your contribution chart, you see even more information from each of your connected networks. You can use this table to view information like your number of followers, likes, and mentions on your various networks, and determine your strengths and weaknesses therein (see Figure 3-6).

You can use the arrows on the left and right sides of the Stats section to scroll to more information.

🐦 Twitter	📘 Facebook	🔴 Google+
💬 800+ Mentions	♥ 500+ Friends	💬 30+ +1s
💬 100+ Lists	♥ 700+ Likes	💬 10+ Comments
💬 90+ Retweets	💬 200+ Comments	♥ 3+ Reshares
♥ 2K+ Followers	💬 30+ Wall Posts	Info is gathered from public posts only.

Figure 3-6: Network statistics at a glance.

Your network statistics are measured from only those posts and comments that are publicly shared. Private comments or information isn't calculated in these numbers. If your Twitter account is public, all of your posts will be included in your score. Facebook, however, allows you to be selective each time you post an update. If you wish to mark an update as public, make sure to select this option in your status update before posting.

Comparing your Score with other influencers

If you want to compare your Score with another influencer, simply enter her name into the search bar at the top of any page on Klout and view her profile page to see her Klout Score.

Further, if you want to compare your Score with other influencers in a certain topic of influence, search for that topic using the search bar and a list of the top influencers for that subject and their Klout Scores appear.

Sharing your Score

When you log in to Klout, you may see a pop-up window with a report of how your score is performing. Within this window is the option to share your current Score via Twitter or Facebook. To share, simply click the button for the network you wish to use, and a pre-written message will populate in the share window. You may use this message or create your own.

You can always create your own status updates via your social networks or share information using the Twitter and Facebook sharing buttons located in your profile.

Discovering Klout Moments

Klout Moments are a great way to see how your community reacts to what you share. After you have scrolled through your Score statistics, the rest of your Dashboard is dedicated to your most influential Moments — updates, tweets, photos, and the like that spark engagement in your online community — across your connected networks for the most recent 90-day period.

You can view your Klout Moments from either your Dashboard or Profile page within Klout. (I tell you about the latter option in

Chapter 4.) Each list gives a different set of information about your social engagement in your various networks. Klout Moments currently pull data from Facebook, Twitter, Google+, and Klout.

When you view your Moments from your Dashboard, you get a bit more detail about each post.

Click the Home button in the navigation bar at the top of the screen on Klout. If you've turned Show Stats on, scroll past your stats to locate your most influential Moments from the most recent 90-day period. If Show Stats is off, as shown in Figure 3-7, your most influential Moments appear near the top of the page.

Figure 3-7: Viewing Klout Moments on your Dashboard.

Klout offers a few different ways to observe your most influential Moments in the Dashboard. Your most recent interactions are arranged at the top of the list and go in reverse chronological order from there.

When you look at your Moments, you notice the following elements:

✓ **Social network:** The icon for the social network from which a Moment was pulled appears on the left side of your screen next to the post. You can click this icon to go to the original post on its corresponding network (such as Twitter or Facebook).

✔ **Your post:** When you click a post that's displayed on your Dashboard, you see the original date and time in the upper-right corner of your post, along with five dots that are used to assign a rating to your post based on the amount of interaction it received, with five dots indicating a high amount of engagement.

✔ **Interactions:** To show all of the interactions for a moment, click the phrase View More at the right of that moment. A pop-up window appears, as shown in Figure 3-8.

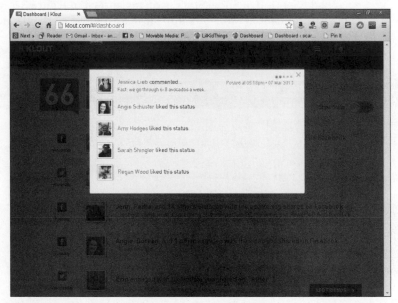

Figure 3-8: Expanded interactions for a Klout Moment.

By reviewing your Klout Moments via your profile as well as your Dashboard, you can collect useful data to improve the quality of the way you share information with your community.

Chapter 4

Navigating Your Klout Profile Page

In This Chapter

▶ Checking out your profile page

▶ Connecting with other influencers

▶ Inviting friends to join Klout

*Y*ou can access your Klout profile page by clicking Profile on the navigation bar at the top of the screen. On this page, you see a snapshot of recent activity (Klout Moments), your connected networks, your bio, your influencers, and your topics. This is also the page the public sees when they view your profile within Klout. This chapter highlights the important tools on your profile page and tells you how to use them to get the most out of Klout.

Learning the Lay of the Land

When you look at your profile page, you see your photo, your name, and your Klout Score in the upper-left corner of the screen. Directly below your photo, you see an interactive series of icons. These icons represent the networks you have connected to Klout.

For example, I have connected Twitter, Facebook, Google+, LinkedIn, YouTube, Instagram, Blogger, and Flickr to Klout (see Figure 4-1). Therefore, my Score is in part based upon my ability to promote engagement in these networks.

If you are like me and have many networks connected, they are not all displayed. You can show more icons by mousing over the plus sign at the right of your list of icons as shown in Figure 4-2.

Figure 4-1: My connected networks.

Reveal more networks

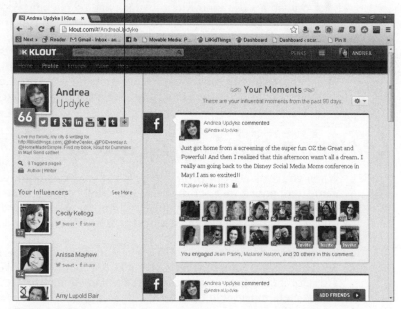

Figure 4-2: Show more icons.

Clicking on any of these icons takes your browser to the corresponding social network (such as Twitter, Facebook, and so on). Likewise, when others view your Klout page, they also have the option to click through and connect with you on these other social media sites.

You can add or remove a network to Klout at any time by mousing over your name in the upper-right corner of the screen and selecting Settings from the drop-down menu. Choose Connected Networks to add or remove networks as desired. (In Chapter 7, I give you more details about how to connect additional networks.)

When you created your account, you either created a bio or allowed Klout to use the bio that appears on your Twitter account. This bio is shown under your name and connected networks on your page.

I decided to use my Twitter bio when I created my account. You can see it populated in Figure 4-3.

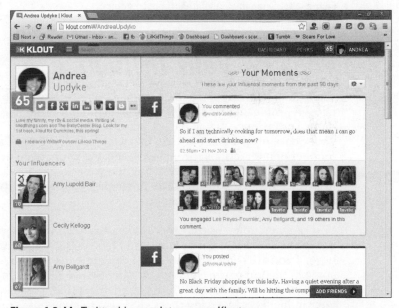

Figure 4-3: My Twitter bio populates on my Klout page.

If you have connected LinkedIn to Klout, you see a link below your bio, as shown in Figure 4-4. This link takes people directly to your LinkedIn profile page.

Linking to your LinkedIn account

Figure 4-4: My job title populated from LinkedIn.

Showcasing Your Influence

Your Klout Score appears in an orange box overlaid on your chosen profile picture. This is a dynamic number that can change daily. For instance, if you have a period of inactivity, you might see your Score drop a point or two. Likewise, when you have a high number of interactions (or engagement) via your social networks like Twitter and Facebook, you may see your Score increase. The more engagement you generate, the higher your Score. This is the measure of your online influence.

You can view some of your top influencers from your Klout page as well as compare your Scores, and I tell you how you can do that here. If you are trying to increase your Score, it's helpful to review some of the top performers in your niche to identify ways you can improve your own Score. While you're doing that, you can endorse your influencers by giving them +K. I also tell you how you can find out within which topic areas you're most influential and request endorsement from people in other social media networks, including Facebook and Twitter.

Locating your influencers

Below your bio and connected network information, you see a list of your top influencers in the sidebar. These are people you connect with on a regular basis via one of your connected networks. These people have been determined by Klout as influential to you based on your engagement with their social network activity. These influencers are listed in order of the highest Klout Score with the highest Score at the top of the list.

You see five influencers in your sidebar. Currently, Klout allows you to see only your top ten influencers. To do so, select the link that says See More that appears to the right of the word *Influencers* at the top of the list as shown in Figure 4-5.

See More

Figure 4-5: The See More button appears as you mouse over your influencer list.

After you select the option to see more, a pop-up box appears showing the top ten people who influence you via your social media accounts (such as Facebook and Twitter).

Influence is defined by Klout as the ability to inspire action. Therefore, the influencers who will likely show up in this list are the people who have inspired you to action (comments, Likes, retweets) in some way.

You have some control over your influencer list. If someone appears in this list that you don't consider particularly influential, you can remove them by hovering over their avatar (picture) and clicking the *x* that appears in the upper-right corner (see Figure 4-6).

Remove an influencer

Figure 4-6: Removing an influencer from your list of top influencers.

Removing someone from your influencer list in Klout won't cause you to stop following them on your other networks (Twitter, Facebook, Google+, and so on).

If you do choose to remove an influencer from your top ten list, you then have the opportunity to replace that person in the list. To do this, click the link at the top of the pop-up box that says Add an Influencer and either type in an individual's name or choose from one of the suggested influencers that appears (see Figure 4-7).

If you do not add someone here, Klout automatically populates the list with the next most influential person from your social networks by Klout Score.

Endorsing other influencers

You can also use your influencer list to make *endorsements,* which is an action Klout describes as giving +K. You can give +K up to 10 times each day. As I mention in Chapter 1, a portion of your Klout Score comes from the number of endorsements you receive from others. Klout puts a limit on the number of endorsements one can give each day in order to maintain the integrity of endorsements, thus leading to a more accurate overall Score.

Figure 4-7: Adding an Influencer to your top ten list.

While you are looking at your top influencer list, you can endorse another influencer by giving +K. Each influencer has her three most influential topics to the right of her name. Select one of these topics and simply click Give +K. Or, if you don't see the topic you're looking for next to the influencer's name, you can view a more comprehensive list by doing the following:

1. **Select the influencer you want to give +K to by clicking on his name.**

   This opens the profile page for that influencer.

2. **Scroll down until you see Topics in the sidebar on the left side of your screen.**

3. **Mouse over the Topics list and click the See More link that appears in the top-right corner of the list.**

4. **Search for the topic you want to choose and Give +K by selecting the orange arrow button to the right of that topic.**

Identifying your influence and requesting +K

The sidebar on your Klout profile page also includes topics of influence based on your social media interactions. Below your top influencers, you see a list of your topics of influence. Like your influencer list, only the highest rated topics are shown.

To see your complete list of topics, select the See More link that appears when you mouse over your topics list. The pop-up box that appears contains all of the topics in which Klout believes you are influential. You can add or remove topics in this list as described in Chapter 6.

Your topics list also lists the last five people who have given you +K in a specific topic as shown in Figure 4-8.

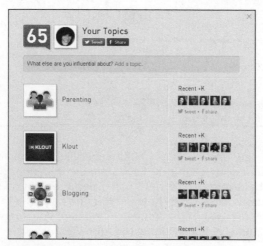

Figure 4-8: Topics of influence and recent +K.

 If you would like to request +K in a particular topic via Facebook or Twitter, you may do so by clicking the corresponding Share button to the right of that topic. You can then share a public request for +K within that account. For instance, if you click the Facebook Share link, your request for +K is posted in your friends' News Feeds.

Inviting Friends to Join Klout

Klout is only as good as the networks you provide. This is why Klout continually improves its service by offering more networks to connect and ways to interact with your influencers, such as giving +K endorsements. In the following sections I tell you how to use Facebook and Twitter to invite friends who haven't yet joined Klout.

Sharing topics and influencers

You may use the Facebook and Twitter Share buttons located in your profile (as mentioned earlier in this chapter) to compose a tweet about Klout. For example, you can click the Facebook or Twitter Share link below your list of influencers or your list of topics (see Figure 4-9) to share some of your influencers or topics of influence with your friends or followers. They then have the option to click the link within your post or tweet and join Klout.

Figure 4-9: Share your influence or topics.

Because you are already connected via Facebook or Twitter, new Klout members are added to your influencer list when they join Klout.

Searching Facebook for influencers

Klout has integrated Facebook invitations in a few different ways. If you would like to use your Facebook account to add friends to Klout, you can use one of the following tools.

Inviting Facebook friends using the Add Friends button

With your Klout profile page displayed, notice the blue tab labeled Add Friends in the bottom-right corner of your browser. This Add Friends tab remains in the same place even as you scroll the content of the page. Click it and you see the Grow Your Influence dialog box shown in Figure 4-10.

Figure 4-10: Add friends to Klout via Facebook.

Notice the two tabs at the top of the box marked Unregistered and All.

- ✔ **Unregistered:** By choosing Unregistered, you have the option to invite only those Facebook friends who aren't already connected to Klout.

- ✔ **All:** Selecting All also includes current Klout members.

Beyond that, each tab is similar. Here you have three options (shown in Figure 4-10) for selecting Facebook friends to invite to Klout:

- ✔ **Select All:** Selecting this check box selects everyone in your friends list to receive an invitation from Klout. Deselecting this box deselects everyone.

- ✔ **Select individual friends:** Your Facebook friends appear in a scrollable list alphabetized by first name. By selecting the check box next to an individual's name, you are agreeing to send them an invitation to Klout. This option allows you to pick and choose who you would like to invite.

- ✔ **Search friends:** Next to the Select All button, you see a search field. This is particularly useful if you are looking for one or two friends to invite and you don't want to scroll through your entire friends list. Start typing a name into the search bar and select the check box that appears next to your friend's name to invite.

After you have made your selections, click the orange Continue button. This opens another pop-up screen that contains your Facebook authorization and a preview of your invitation. If everything looks the way you want it to, click Send Request (as shown in Figure 4-11).

Figure 4-11: Facebook invitation request authorization.

You then see a notification on your screen that says Invites Sent. Click the *x* in the upper-right corner of the pop-up box to exit the screen.

Inviting Facebook friends from Klout by creating a Wall (Timeline) post

While looking through your various Moments in Klout, you see avatars for your friends who engaged with your post. If your friends are already Klout users, you see their Klout Score overlaid on their avatar. However, if they are not yet connected to Klout, a blue Invite button appears on top of their avatar as shown in Figure 4-12.

Figure 4-12: Klout-connected friends versus those who do not use Klout.

To invite a friend from this screen, click the avatar of the person you wish to invite. This creates a post that appears on your friend's Facebook Wall (Timeline). In the pop-up box that appears, you may customize the message if you wish. Click Share to invite your friend and return to your Klout page (see Figure 4-13).

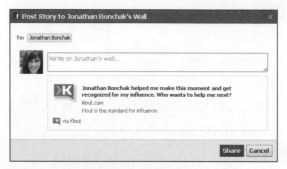

Figure 4-13: Inviting a friend to use Klout using a Facebook Wall (Timeline) post.

Analyzing Your Social Media Engagement

Like in your Dashboard, your profile page also highlights some of your most influential Moments from your various social media accounts. You can display all of the highlighted Moments on your page at once or show only those from a specific network such as Facebook, Twitter, Google+, YouTube, and of course, Klout. Doing so affects only your current view of your Moments. Your followers will see all recent public Moments regardless of network when they view your profile.

The Moments shown here are your top Moments from the most recent 90-day period, including public and private Moments. *Private Moments* (such as posts made to Friends only on your Facebook Timeline) show up only for you or people who are connected with you on Facebook. They are not visible to people who you are not "friends" with on your social networks unless you have the post marked as public within that network.

The posts with the most engagement are at the top of the list. You may view all of your Moments at once or from a specific social network. To sort Moments by social network, click the gear icon in the top-right corner of the Your Moments section of your profile page shown in Figure 4-14. (Your list might be different, depending on which accounts you've connected to Klout.) Choose the desired network from the drop-down menu to view only highlights from that network (such as Facebook).

Figure 4-14: Sorting Moments by social network.

A drop-down menu appears, and you may choose from the following options:

- ✔ **View All Recent Moments:** These Moments include public and private posts from your connected networks with the most engagement within the past 90 days.

- ✔ **View Recent Public Moments:** These posts have the highest engagement from posts you made public on your social networks.

- ✔ **View Recent Twitter Moments:** This option shows only posts via Twitter.

- ✔ **View Recent Facebook Moments:** These posts are only from your Facebook activity.

- ✔ **View Recent Google+ Moments:** This option shows highlighted Moments from your Google+ stream.

- ✔ **View Recent Klout Moments:** A list populates with the most recent K+ you've received from other influencers.

If you would like to view the original post, you may do so by clicking on the time stamp directly under the status update.

 Clicking on any of the avatars with a Klout Score shown in your Klout Moments takes you to the Klout profile page for that influencer.

Chapter 5

Making Influencer Lists

In This Chapter

▶ Organizing your influencers in lists

▶ Publicizing your lists

*M*aking a list is a great way to narrow your influencers into more manageable segments. Within Klout, you can make lists for friends, local businesses, bloggers, and basically anything or anyone you want to group together. Lists can help when you're looking to compare certain interests or Scores or give +K to your friends. The process is simple, as I describe in this chapter, and you can make as many as you want! You can share lists with your social networks or keep them to yourself. At this time, Klout doesn't display your lists to people who view your Profile.

Managing Lists

You can find your lists by selecting Friends from the navigation bar at the top of your screen. After you are on your Friends page, take a look at the sidebar on the left side of your screen (shown in Figure 5-1). You see the option to view your Facebook and Twitter friends separately. Below those options is where your personal lists are. If you don't yet have any lists, you can create them here.

Creating a list

In the sidebar on the left side of your Friends screen, you see an orange Create a New List button. When you click this button, a pop-up window appears, as shown in Figure 5-2. In this box, you can add people to the list and name the list.

Figure 5-1: Your lists appear on the left side of the Friends page.

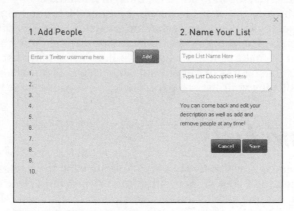

Figure 5-2: Create a new list.

At this time, you can only add influencers by their Twitter name. To create a list, follow these steps:

1. **To add an influencer to your list, type her Twitter name into the provided field and push enter.**

   When you're typing Twitter names, you don't need to include the @ symbol.

2. **Continue adding people to your list.**

   After you've finished adding users to your list, create a list name in the provided field on the right side of the pop-up window.

   3. **Click the List Name text box and type the list name.**

   You may add a description if you so desire below your list
   name.

   4. **(Optional) Click the Description text box and type a
   description.**

   5. **Click the orange Save button to create your list and close
   the pop-up window.**

Your new list appears in the sidebar on the left side of your screen
as shown in Figure 5-3.

Figure 5-3: A new list (Brands Who Get It) has been created.

Adding and removing influencers in your existing lists

Updating your lists is easy. After you've created a list, you can add
or remove people at any time. All you need is their Twitter name.

To add users to an existing list, go to your Friends page and do the
following:

   1. **Select the list you wish to edit by clicking the name in the
   sidebar.**

   Your list appears in the main section of your page, as
   shown in Figure 5-4.

Figure 5-4: Your existing list appears on your Friends page.

2. **Scroll to the bottom of the page and click the orange Edit This List button.**

   A pop-up box appears.

3. **Add more users to your list by typing their Twitter name in the provided field.**

4. **Click the Save button to update your list and return to your Friends page.**

To remove users from an existing list, follow these steps:

1. **Select the list you wish to edit by clicking the name in the sidebar.**

   Your list appears in the main section of your page.

2. **Scroll to the bottom of the page and click the orange Edit This List button.**

   A pop-up box appears.

3. **Hover over the name of the user you wish to delete until an *x* appears next to his name, as seen in Figure 5-5.**

4. **Click the *x* to remove this user from your list.**

5. **To save this action and return to your Friends page, click the Save button.**

Figure 5-5: An *x* appears when you hover the mouse over a name in your list.

Deleting your list

If you've created a list you no longer wish to keep, you can delete it at any time. Deleting a list is simple. Navigate to your Friends page by hovering over your name in the upper-right corner of Klout.com and select Friends from the drop-down list that appears.

When on your Friends page, select the list you wish to delete by clicking the name in the sidebar on the left side of your screen. Scroll to the bottom of the list and click the blue Delete This List button.

A pop-up confirmation appears (as shown in Figure 5-6). If you're sure you want to delete your list, click the Okay button, and your list disappears.

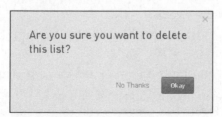

Figure 5-6: Confirm that you'd like to delete the list.

Building Influence through List Sharing

Whether you want to build your online influence or just have fun using your various social media networks, Klout lists can help you do both. You can use the Lists feature to create meaningful, well-curated collections of influencers that your followers will be drawn to.

For instance, if you blog about music, you might consider making lists of your favorite up-and-coming musicians, local bands, or record labels. You can share these lists via Facebook, Twitter, and LinkedIn, and your followers can then add these lists to their own pages and use them to find new accounts to follow.

In short, anything you can do to make yourself the go-to resource on a particular topic only increases the value of your influence. Using Klout lists to place like-minded influencers together in one easy-to-follow place is a great way to share some of your knowledge with your followers for free. Everybody wins!

 Many social networks use pop-up windows to complete sharing actions. Make sure you allow pop-ups within your browser to use the share features.

Twitter sharing

To share your list via Twitter, go to your Friends page and follow these steps:

1. **Open your list by clicking the name in the sidebar on the left side of your screen.**

   After your list is open, you see social share buttons in the upper-right corner of the screen.

2. **Click the Twitter button to open the share pop-up box.**

   A Twitter message box appears with a pre-written message as shown in Figure 5-7. You may edit this message or send it as-is.

3. **Click the Tweet button to send your tweet and return to your Friends page.**

Figure 5-7: Share your list via Twitter.

Facebook sharing

Sharing your list via Facebook is easy. When you share in this way, Klout creates a Facebook Wall (Timeline) post that's visible to anyone who views your Facebook Timeline or your News Feed. From there, when they click your link, they are directed to Klout.

To share a list with Facebook, go to your Friends page and follow these steps:

1. **Open your list by clicking the name in the sidebar on the left side of your screen.**

2. **Click the Facebook button from the social sharing buttons in the upper-right side of your screen.**

   A pop-up box with your Facebook post appears as shown in Figure 5-8.

3. **You may customize your Wall (Timeline) post by typing in the provided message field or post the update with no additional text.**

4. **Click the Share button to post this message to your Facebook Timeline and return to your Klout Friends page.**

If you don't wish to share your Klout link with everyone who views your Facebook Timeline, you have the option (as explained in the list that follows) to customize your audience within Facebook. This option might be helpful if you want to engage only a certain group of friends or business contacts.

Figure 5-8: Share your list via Facebook.

To customize your Facebook message recipients, follow the above instructions through Step 3 to create your Wall (Timeline) post. Then use the following steps to customize the recipients of your post.

1. **To the left of the blue Facebook Share button, you'll notice a small Privacy button with an arrow. Click this button to customize the Facebook friends who see your update (shown in Figure 5-9).**

2. **Choose the group of people with whom you'd like to share the list.**

   - *Public:* The default setting will match your privacy settings in Facebook. If you wish to publicly share your list, select the globe icon to make your Wall (Timeline) post visible to anyone whether or not you are Facebook friends.

   - *Friends:* Select the icon with the people on it to share your post with all of your Facebook friends.

   - *Custom:* Choose the gear icon to customize your recipients by name or network and select from one of the available options when the Custom Privacy dialog box appears (shown in Figure 5-10).

     To share your post with a specific network, select the check box for the appropriate network and click Save Changes.

To share your post with only specific individuals, choose Make This Post Visible To specific people or lists from the drop-down menu and type in each person's name that you wish to see your post and click Save Changes.

- *List:* Notice that you might have additional selections, depending on how your Facebook account is set up. Within your Facebook account, you can set up customized lists of people so that you can quickly and easily choose who sees your posts. Setting up Facebook lists is beyond the scope of this book, but you can consult the Facebook Help Center for more information.

Figure 5-9: Customize your Facebook share recipients.

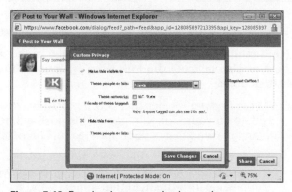

Figure 5-10: Facebook custom sharing options.

3. **After you have made your desired sharing selections, click the Share button to complete your Facebook post and return to your Klout Friends page.**

Sharing via LinkedIn

To share your list via your LinkedIn account, follow these steps:

1. **Open your list by clicking the name in the sidebar on the left side of your screen.**

2. **Select the LinkedIn button from the social share buttons in the top-right corner of your Friends page.**

   A pop-up box appears (Figure 5-11).

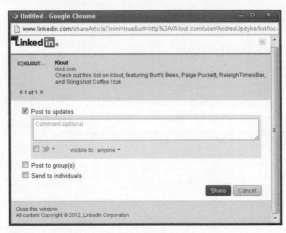

Figure 5-11: Share your list via LinkedIn.

You can share the list as-is or customize your LinkedIn post.

3. **(Optional) If you'd like to add a message in the provided field or choose from the following options, follow these instructions.**

   • *Post to Updates:* Select this check box to make a status update on your LinkedIn page. This post will be visible to anyone who views your updates on LinkedIn.

   • *Post to Groups:* Select this check box to select a specific group to whom you want to send your post. Type the group name into the field that appears and a message if desired.

- *Send to Individuals:* Select this check box to send your list to specific connections on LinkedIn. Type each person's name into the provided field and a message if desired.

4. **Select the blue Share button to share your list and return to your Friends page.**

You may select any or all of the options to share via LinkedIn. Remember to deselect the check boxes for sharing options you don't wish to use so you don't inadvertently spam your connections!

Chapter 6

Identifying Your Klout Topics

A s Klout scans your various social media activity, the site identifies certain themes that tend to inspire the most engagement among your followers. These themes are called your *topics of influence* and appear on your Klout profile page.

If you're using Klout to identify ways to grow your online community and your influence, keeping an eye on your topics is a great way to see what your followers are responding to. This is not an exact science of course, but simply a way to peek through the lens and see which topics encourage the most engagement from your followers, as I discuss in this chapter.

Targeting Your Online Influence

When I open my Klout profile and look at my top three topics of influence, I can see that they are Parenting, Klout, and Blogging, as shown in Figure 6-1. This makes perfect sense for me because I am a parenting blogger and I'm writing this book. Because I'm using my social media accounts as a part of my business, I want these topics to be relevant to my business. In the same way, if you're trying to increase your online influence in a certain topic, use your online accounts to discuss things related to that topic.

For instance, if you wish to be influential in the topic of cars, you will do well to discuss news in the automotive industry, vehicles you love, and whatever other aspects of this topic you enjoy.

Figure 6-1: My top three Klout topics of influence.

Evaluating your topics of influence

Klout uses a few ways to determine the topics in which it believes you to be influential. One way is to scan the engagement you inspire across your various social media networks. Often this can provide an accurate representation of your influence. However, this isn't always the most reliable way to gauge influence. For instance, during the Discovery Channel's Shark Week series of TV shows, I was using Twitter to discuss what I was watching. A few days later, Klout determined that I was influential about the topic of sharks, which couldn't be further from the truth because they terrify me!

For this reason, Klout allows you to add and remove up to 20 topics of influence, and I tell you how to do that later in this chapter. This way, if a rogue topic gets thrown into the mix, you can simply delete it and move on. Of course, if you're using social media for recreation, it can be a lot of fun to go through the list and see a profile of your recent social media interactions.

Building social media consistency

When you're using social media for business purposes, it's a necessary evil to consider social media strategy. Of course you don't want to alienate your followers with spam and insincere posts, but you need to be mindful of the niche you're trying to promote and filter your posts through that lens, so to speak.

Some ideas to consider when building social media consistency include

- ✔ **Connecting with your followers:** Ask a question each week that inspires action and relates to your brand. You could ask the same question each week, or change it up.

- ✔ **Responding to comments:** When it comes to brands on social media, the most successful are the ones who seem relatable and human. Answer questions, respond to posts, and boost your brand's image.

- ✔ **Resolving complaints:** Silence is never golden on the internet when it comes to brand complaints. If there is an issue or a complaint, always respond publicly. You don't have to divulge details, but when something negative appears, your followers need to know that someone is working to resolve the issue. Many people who don't comment are still lurking and watching to see how a brand deals with conflict.

For a great example of someone who's good at using social media to cultivate friendships while at the same time building her brand, look at Katja Presnal of the blog Skimbacolifestyle.com (Figure 6-2). Katja engages users from all over the world to share their beautiful photographs (via Instagram and Twitter) using the hashtag #skimbaco, which is a term Katja created to represent living life to the fullest.

Figure 6-2: Skimbaco Lifestyle blog — a modern-day carpe diem.

In doing this, Katja is not only inspiring her audience to live life to the fullest, but also to share it with their own communities. She is consistently raising awareness about her brand while giving her followers a way to share the things that make them happy (see Figure 6-3). This is the sweet spot of social media strategy.

Figure 6-3: Instagram photos tagged with the #skimbaco hashtag.

Discussing topics within your niche

If you're targeting a specific niche, you need to have a certain level of consistency when you post on your social media networks. This does not have to be constricting, however. It just means that you are conscious of your brand message as you are posting. Keep in mind that many of your followers are like-minded individuals who want to see updates that are relevant to your common interests.

Use different forms of media to create interest and still stay on point. Video, images, and storytelling convey your message in an interesting and diverse way while drawing readers back to your message.

Make Klout lists of like-minded influencers and share some of their work with your readers. Doing so increases your authenticity on a particular topic and benefits those influencers who may reciprocate the gesture.

Managing Your Topics

To view and manage your Klout topics, point your browser to Klout.com and select Profile from the drop-down that appears when you click your name in the upper-right corner of the screen. In this section, I tell you how to find what Klout thinks are your most influential areas, delete any of those if you'd like, and add even more topics.

Finding your topics

Your top three topics of influence are located in the sidebar on the left of your screen when viewing your Klout profile page. However, you can have up to 20 topics of influence. To view all of your topics of influence, click the See More link next to your topics list (shown in Figure 6-4). A pop up-window appears.

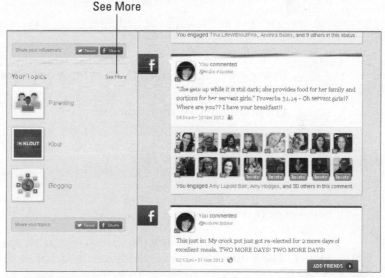

Figure 6-4: Click See More to view all of your Klout topics.

Deleting your topics

If you want to delete topics in your list, you can do so easily:

1. **Open your topics list by clicking the See More link located to the right of your top three topics.**

2. **Click the Manage Your Topics link that appears in the top-right corner (see Figure 6-5).**

Manage Your Topics

Figure 6-5: Manage topics to make changes. _____

3. **Delete a topic by mousing over a topic and clicking the *x* that appears.**

4. **Click Save to save your changes.**

Adding more topics

You can add topics to your topics list as well. This is particularly helpful if you are new to social media or are creating a new account or branching out.

After a topic is created, other influencers see it as an option to give you +K. The more +K you get on a topic, the higher on the list it appears.

To add a topic to Klout, do the following:

1. **Open your topics list by clicking the See More link next to your top three topics in the sidebar.**

2. **Click Manage Your Topics in the upper-right corner of the window that appears.**

3. **Choose a topic from the list of suggestions or add your own by clicking Add a Topic at the top of the window (see Figure 6-6).**

Add a Topic

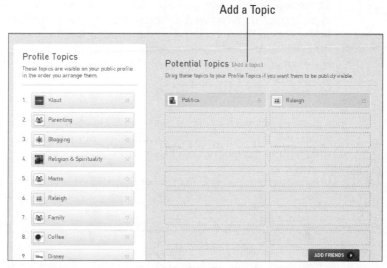

Figure 6-6: Add a topic to your Klout profile.

4. **Type the new topic into the field provided and click add.**

5. **Drag the topic from the list of Potential Topics to the column titled Profile Topics.**

6. **Click Save.**

Only ten topics will be visible in your public profile. However, you can keep more topics in your Potential Topics column and rotate them out if your interests change.

Finding Influencers by Topic

Finding new people to follow by using Klout is a great way to increase your community. Because you can search by topic, as I explain in this section, Klout allows you to hone in on specific ideas to build your community. This can be a great tool when you're working on a specific project or want to target a specific market within the online community.

Searching for influencers

You may find that you want to search for Influencers by topic. These are users who are influential in that topic and have a demonstrated online influence in that topic based on their social media engagement. To search a topic, type it into the search bar at the top of your screen and then press Enter. A results page appears.

At the top of this page, you may see a list of users with that topic in their user name as well as the top influencers for that topic. Below this, a list of recent, top moments appears.

For example, if I want to find people who are influential on the topic of Raleigh, North Carolina, which is where I live, I type **Raleigh** into the search box at the top of my screen and press Enter.

A page opens with one user named @Raleigh, a list of the top influencers for the topic, "Raleigh", and a list of moments about Raleigh with high engagement (see Figure 6-7).

People matching "raleigh"

Raleigh Weather (@Raleigh)
Weather updates, forecast, warnings and information for Raleigh, NC. Sources: WeatherBug, NOAA, USGS.

Top influencers for "raleigh"

New Raleigh   RaleighNews   Goodnight Ralei.

Crash Gregg   newsobserver.c.   RaleighTimesBar

Indy Week   TBJ Raleigh/Du.   NC Museum of..

See all influencers

Top moments for "raleigh" (From the past 90 days)   ADD FRIENDS ▶

See All Influencers

Figure 6-7: Searching for influencers about Raleigh, North Carolina.

You can view more influencers by clicking See All Influencers located under the partial list that shows up on the results page. Likewise, to view more Moments, scroll to the bottom of the page and select Show More.

Following like-minded influencers

Using the Topics feature to find like-minded influencers you might not otherwise have known about helps you build your online community and increase your social reach. You might even want to create a list for a certain topic (which I tell you how to do in Chapter 5) and share it with your followers.

By curating like-minded groups of influencers and sharing them with your existing followers, you grow in your own influence on that topic.

Anytime you can give your followers something useful for free — such as a list of influential people to follow — is only going to increase your value as an online influencer.

Chapter 7

Increasing Your Klout Score

*1*f there is one thing you should remember while reading this book, it's that your Klout Score is just a number. There are many ways to measure your influence both on and offline. Looking at your Klout Score is one way to measure certain aspects of that influence. I like to use it as a personal metric of growth, sort of like stepping on a bath scale. Of course, with a scale measuring my weight, I want the numbers to go down, but when it comes to my Klout Score, the higher the better!

Klout measures influence on a scale of 1 to 100 with the average user having a Score of 40. And although Klout uses many different data points to reach what it believes to be accurate Scores, don't get terribly wrapped up in the number. At the end of the day, as an online influencer, you want to create engagement because of the quality of your content, not your Klout Score. That said, when your content is great, your Klout Score will likely follow suit. In this chapter, I give you some tips on how to improve your content, engage readers, and increase your Klout Score.

Connecting More Social Networks to Klout

Making the most of your social networks improves your Klout Score only if your networks are connected to Klout. The Klout Score is currently based on activity within Facebook, Google+, Twitter, Klout, LinkedIn, Wikipedia, and foursquare, but Klout plans to include more variables in its scoring in the future.

You can connect additional networks to Klout now if you wish. Even though they may not yet count toward your Score, by connecting them to Klout, you're giving anyone who views your profile the ability to click through to all of your networks and follow your social activity.

To connect your social networks to Klout, do the following:

1. **Log in to Klout.com by connecting via Twitter or Facebook.**

2. **Click your name in the upper-right corner of the screen and select Settings from the drop-down menu that appears.**

3. **On the Settings page, choose Connected Networks from the list of options in the sidebar on the left of the screen (shown in Figure 7-1).**

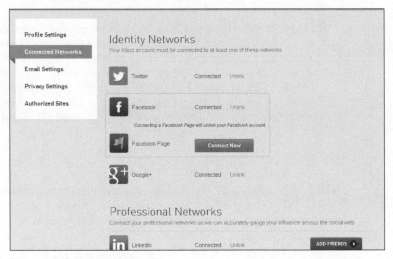

Figure 7-1: Connected Networks.

On the Connected Networks page, you see that the networks are segmented into three categories: Identity Networks, Professional Networks, and Additional Networks. Currently, the only networks that count toward your Klout Score are the Identity and Professional networks.

4. **Select the network you wish to connect to and click the Connect Now button to the right of the network name.**

You are directed to the network page (Twitter or Facebook, for example).

5. **If you aren't already signed in to that network, log in with your username and password as shown in Figure 7-2.**

Figure 7-2: You must log in to your social network to complete Klout authorization.

To authorize Klout to connect to your network, allow it in whatever network you are connecting (shown in Figure 7-3).

6. **If you agree to this, click Allow and return to Klout.**

Figure 7-3: Allow your various social networks to connect with Klout.

You have the option to share this new connection via Twitter and Facebook. Doing so creates a status update on your Facebook or Twitter stream with a link back to your Klout profile.

It can take 24 to 48 hours for your new network to be added to Klout, so don't worry if you don't see it right away!

Building Quality Online Content

Remember that Klout defines *influence* as the ability to drive action. You don't need an algorithm to determine whether or not your social media updates are driving action. All you have to do is take a look at a snapshot (like your Klout Moments shown in Figure 7-4) of a few days of interactions and see for yourself. Klout tells you how many people engaged with your content.

Figure 7-4: Klout Moments.

The social media actions that Klout considers when calculating your influence can take on many different forms, serve different purposes, and are all valuable to Klout when calculating your Score. Those social media actions may include the following:

- ✔ **Likes:** When you get Likes, favorites, or +1s across your various social networks (Twitter, Facebook, and Google+), it tells Klout that people are reading your content and responding.

- ✔ **Shares:** Shares and retweets are the ultimate compliment. Not only did someone enjoy your content for himself, he thought his own followers would also enjoy it, which could potentially bring new eyes to your content.

- ✔ **Comments:** Asking questions on your social networks is a great way to create engagement. Comments can spark new conversations and even lead to future blog posts.

When you're thinking about how you can best build quality online content, consider how often you post content, when, and how others respond to it. You might observe some trends that can help you decide how to create more successful content in your social media accounts.

Updating social networks consistently

The Internet is a big place with a constant stream of information. It can be easy to feel lost or unimportant no matter how big or small your network. A good rule to remember is that quality not quantity is what truly matters. This is not only true for your community, but Klout actually factors it into its scoring algorithm.

For instance, if you have a high number of followers, but only a small percentage are engaging with you, your Score might not be as high as someone with half the number of followers who are all commenting and sharing regularly.

Likewise, if an influencer posts 20 updates and 5 of those posts get great engagement, she won't get as much credit as someone who posts 10 times a day with 5 posts getting great engagement.

In other words, simply being active won't raise your Klout Score. Engagement is king. And the key to engagement is creating quality content.

However, being present in the social media space is also important. You don't want to disappear for long periods of time. Updating your social networks with consistency creates a feeling of permanence and reliability that leads to your readers looking forward to your updates.

Observing trends in your popular posts

To get an idea of the types of posts that get the most interactions, take a look at your Klout Moments. You can view your Moments either in your Klout Dashboard or your profile page (as explained in Chapter 3). For the best engagement overview from my followers however, I prefer the Dashboard view.

Observe engagement by viewing Klout Moments in your Dashboard with these steps:

1. **Locate your Dashboard by logging in to Klout.com and clicking Home on the navigation bar at the top of the page.**

Your most influential recent Moments are in the main section of your Dashboard (shown in Figure 7-5).

Figure 7-5: Your Klout Moments via your Dashboard.

Moments are organized by date and social network with the original post in the main window and the comments and Likes to the right of the post.

2. **Click the View More arrow to the right of a listing to see all of the engagement for a particular Moment, as shown in Figure 7-6.**

As you're reviewing your engagement, take a few things into consideration for the future, as noted in Figure 7-7. Was your post humorous? Was it text only or did it include a link or a picture? What time of day was it? Did you ask a question? On which social network was it posted?

All of this information can be valuable to you for future use. Look for trends in your posts. You might find that your followers tend to respond more in the morning hours or when you post on Facebook rather than other networks such as Twitter or Google+. Of course, this doesn't mean you ignore the afternoon or those other networks. It simply means you should maximize your efforts during your peak hours. These are the times you want to post so you can have your words in front of as many eyes as possible.

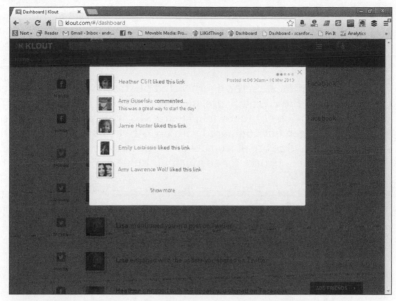

Figure 7-6: Expanded view of engagement on a particular post.

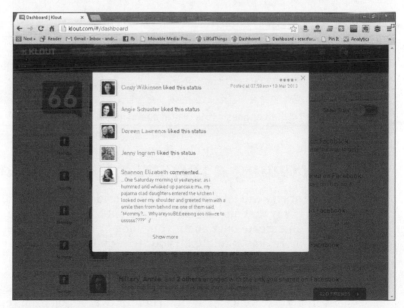

Figure 7-7: The content of a post with quality engagement.

As a parenting blogger, my community is full of other parents who share a similar schedule whether they work outside of the home or stay home with their kids. The bulk of my social media interactions happen either in the early morning hours or just after lunch, otherwise known as nap time. Your peak times will depend on your community. Think of observing trends as a form of listening to your followers. Everybody wins.

Sometimes it's the lighthearted posts that get the most feedback. After the 2012 U.S. presidential election, I decided to post about my Crock-Pot (shown in Figure 7-8). This post got a great deal of engagement compared with my other posts that week. I think it was a nice break from all of the political banter that flooded the social networks for so much of the year.

Figure 7-8: Humor goes a long way in social media.

Becoming a resource to your readers

Authenticity will take you far in the world of social media. Most experts say that although it's important to get your message out there and create buzz about your blog or business, it's equally, if not more, important to be your true and authentic self when online. After all, social media is supposed to be social!

This doesn't mean you have to share all of life's little details, however; people are using the Internet for everything from recipes to reading the news to making friends, and becoming a resource to your community is a great way to not only help your friends, but also to keep you and your brand front and center in their minds when they do need something.

Be a connector. We all have our go-to people for when we have questions about certain topics. If you can establish your brand and yourself as a go-to person, people will seek you out for tips and encouragement.

For example, I am friends with a local couple who are in the coffee industry. They are naturally fun and social and it shows through their social network interactions. But they also consistently post updates with interesting facts about coffee, where to get great coffee, or local festivals that feature their coffee (shown in Figure 7-9).

Figure 7-9: Slingshot Coffee Company's Facebook Page Updates.

They are a great team and although they each work for different companies and work to promote their brands, they also support the coffee industry as a whole, even if it means mentioning a competitor now and again. As a reader and fellow coffee lover, I trust their opinion because of their willingness and ability to share their expertise with anyone who will listen. That makes them my go-to people when I want to learn how to make great coffee.

Some ways you can establish yourself as a resource are to

✔ **Curate a list of favorites.** No matter what your niche is online, everyone has to eat. You could create a blog post or Pinterest board (shown in Figure 7-10) with your favorite recipes to share with your followers. Chances are they'll respond by sharing their favorites!

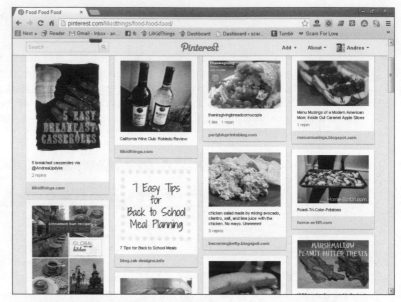

Figure 7-10: A recipe board on Pinterest.

✔ **Use your Klout lists to stimulate conversation on your followers' favorite topics.** Create conversation with your followers by asking who they would add to the list. Give your list some limitations like the top 20 and announce monthly updates to keep the conversation going. (See Figure 7-11.)

Figure 7-11: Local retailers in Raleigh.

✓ **Make a list of Twitter users you think your readers would enjoy.** It could be anyone from comedians to parenting experts. Your Twitter followers can then subscribe to your list (shown in Figure 7-12) and find new influencers to learn from.

Figure 7-12: A Twitter list of book bloggers and authors by Andrea @Gr8Thoughts.

Communicating Great Content

Even if you use your social media networks as a part of your job or business plan, being social is genuinely fun. So have fun with it! You are promoting your ideas and creating buzz on a regular basis, but don't forget to pay it forward. Remember all those Likes, comments, and shares that you hope to receive? When you generously dole them out to other influencers, they'll remember. Many times they'll even return the favor. And don't forget that as you engage with others, your network sees that content as well. Just like the old adage says, it's better to give than to receive.

It can be easy to get bogged down in the business side of content creation. But if you're like me, you got into this business because you loved it. Take a few moments to read and promote someone else's work. You might even get inspired in the process.

Using social media truly is a conversation. When you keep the conversation going organically, your Klout Score reacts accordingly. There is no such thing as too much conversation.

Sharing quality online content

When you're reading blogs and checking out brand websites, take a few moments to make note of the ones that stand out. Then share these with your readers at various times throughout the week. Some articles you'll want to share right away. Still others you may like not for a specific article but because of the whole experience of visiting the website. When you discover great content and share it with your followers, you become a resource.

Don't forget to link to the websites you're promoting and if you want to use one of its images, ask permission first! Most people are happy to share.

Here are some suggestions for sharing web content you love:

✔ **Highlight a new blog or brand each week** (as shown in Figure 7-13) on your Facebook page and link to one of your favorite posts from the previous week. Ask bloggers to submit ideas for new blogs and share the love!

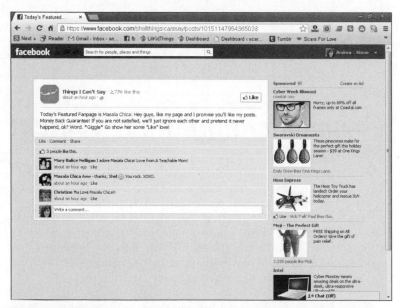

Figure 7-13: Blogger of the week.

✔ **Use the Follow Friday trend on Twitter** and make it personal. Instead of throwing a bunch of names in a tweet and adding the #FollowFriday hashtag (Figure 7-14), select three twitter

accounts to highlight each week and give a brief description
of why your followers would benefit from checking out their
work. Remember to use the #FollowFriday or #FF hashtags in
each tweet.

Figure 7-14: Using the Follow Friday hashtag on Twitter.

> ✔ **Create a blog post with a round-up of items you think would
> be of interest to your readers** (shown in Figure 7-15). Perhaps
> it's a list of social media experts, favorite recipes, or crafts
> you can do with your children. Maybe you're planning a trip
> and you want to showcase different locations that you want to
> visit. Whatever it is, have fun with it!

Choosing which Facebook account to connect

If you have both a Facebook profile (using your name) and a Facebook Page (with
your blog name), you can currently connect only one of these to Klout. If having a
higher Klout Score is one of your goals, you would do better to connect the page/
profile that has the most engagement.

If you have your personal profile set to private, only your Facebook friends see your
interactions when they view your Klout profile.

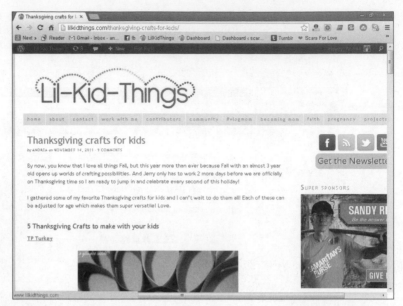

Figure 7-15: Round-up of Thanksgiving crafts for kids on Lilkidthings.com.

Interacting via social networks

As I mentioned earlier, using your social media networks to build conversation is not only fun, it's good business. When you engage with your followers, they are more likely to engage with you. You can naturally communicate by asking questions and offering sincere feedback to others.

Commenting authentically

There is something to be said about genuine social interaction. It can seem overwhelming to respond to every single post directed your way, so don't try! Just as quality trumps quantity, make sure your comments are natural and organic, not forced.

Just like a face-to-face conversation, people can tell when someone isn't being sincere online. As your followers increase and you find yourself having online conversations, try to remember that a real person is on the other end of that keyboard.

When you're reading other blog posts and status updates, an authentic comment goes a long way. Likewise, when people comment on your own updates, take a moment to respond to them or say thanks if they give a compliment to you.

In other words, be real. Be human. Be appreciative.

Creating conversation

Sometimes online interaction can be awkward. Even in a community, people get shy and you may find that you need to draw them out a bit. You can do this a few ways and create some fun conversations in the process.

- ✔ **Ask a question.** Whether on your blog, Facebook Page, Twitter account, or LinkedIn profile, questions are a natural way to get people talking. For example, our coffee maker recently broke, so I took to my Facebook Page asking for recommendations (see Figure 7-16). The conversation exploded with tips, jokes, and conversation between people who only have me as a common bond. It was really fun to watch and be a part of!

Figure 7-16: A great conversation stemming from one simple question on Facebook.

- ✔ **Share a clever photograph or quote.** Another way to get people talking is to share a meaningful or inspiring quote. A little encouragement goes a long way even on the Internet. You never know just what someone needs to hear (or see).

- ✔ **Reference another conversation.** If you were involved in a great conversation on someone else's blog post or page, keep it going! Refer to the post with a link in your status update and introduce new people to the topic. Not only are you paying it forward by linking to another influencer's content, but you're also involving your own community in the discussion.

If you share content from someone else, give her credit and link back to the original source. This is not just common courtesy; it's copyright law. Don't steal.

Giving and Receiving +K

As previously mentioned, giving Klout (called +K) to another influencer is a means of endorsing them in a particular topic. Klout takes these endorsements into consideration when calculating each influencer's Score up to a certain amount that's capped within a 90-day period.

You can give +K on up to ten topics each day. You have the option to give all ten to one influencer or spread it around to ten different users. Giving +K to other influencers lets them know they're doing a great job. In the world of social media, you don't get a lot of performance reviews. For this reason, I like to be generous with +K because everyone needs a little boost sometimes.

Naturally, you're probably curious about who has given you +K, so I tell you how to find that information as well.

Giving +K to another influencer

To give +K to another influencer, you must be logged in to Klout. com via your computer or mobile device (Chapter 12). You can endorse another influencer in a couple different places within the Klout website. You can endorse an Influencer via her profile page or a list you've created; you can then endorse someone else via the confirmation box you see after you endorse someone.

It doesn't cost anything to tell people they're doing a great job. And you might just make their day!

To give +K from a list you've created, follow these steps:

1. **Log in to Klout.com by signing in with either your Twitter or Facebook account.**

2. **Select Friends from the navigation menu at the top of the screen.**

3. **On your Friends page, select one of your lists from the sidebar on the left side of the screen.**

   All of the influencers you've added to this list appear in the main column of the page.

   Each influencer has three topics to the right of her name (shown in Figure 7-17). These are the top three topics for which she is believed to be influential.

4. **To give +K in one of these topics, select Give +K on the topic you wish to endorse.**

Figure 7-17: Giving +K within a list.

If you don't see the topic you want to endorse in the top three selected topics, you may choose to view the influencer's profile for more options.

To view all topics for a particular influencer and give +K, do the following:

1. **Make sure you are logged in to Klout.com by connecting with your Twitter or Facebook account.**

2. **Type an influencer's name in the search bar and select them from the list of influencers that appears.**

3. **Scroll down until you see Topics in the sidebar on the left of your screen.**

4. **Mouse over a topic and select the See More link that appears.**

   A pop-up window with a list of topics appears.

5. **Select the topic you wish to endorse by clicking the Give +K button next to the topic.**

   A confirmation appears.

6. **To return to the topics list, close the confirmation box by clicking the *x* in the upper-right corner.**

When viewing your confirmation box, notice that you have the option to share the fact that you gave +K to this influencer via the Twitter and Facebook sharing buttons. Klout also tells you the number of +K you have left to dole out for the day.

If you would like to give +K to more influencers, you can do so right from the confirmation box. After you've given +K to an influencer, a confirmation box appears with the You Have +K Left to Give to Others link.

1. **Click this +K link to continue giving +K.**

   A pop-up box appears with influencer suggestions to endorse.

   Selections are posted at random from your online influencers. This is a quick and easy way to endorse people.

2. **If you agree with the statement, simply click Give +K.**

3. **If you don't want to endorse any of the four people listed, click the Skip button to be given a list of four new influencers and topics (see Figure 7-18).**

Figure 7-18: Use the Skip button to see a new list of influencers.

4. **Continue endorsing until you reach your daily maximum (as shown in Figure 7-19).**

Figure 7-19: Zero +K left to give for the day.

Receiving +K from another influencer

Remember that when you give +K to other influencers, they are likely to return the favor! When you receive +K, it's calculated into your overall Klout Score. Endorsements also provide a way for anyone viewing your Klout profile to see the value your community has placed on you as an influencer.

Your topics are listed in order of the heaviest weight. This is calculated both from your own social media interactions and the endorsements you receive from others.

You can view who has endorsed you with +K by looking at your topics list as well as from your Notifications tab within Klout.com.

To view +K via your topics list

1. **Navigate to your profile page by clicking your name in the upper-right corner of your screen when logged in to Klout.com.**

2. **Scroll down and select the See More link that appears when you mouse over the topics in your sidebar.**

   A pop-up window appears.

   To the right of each topic, you see the avatars for the influencers who gave you the most recent endorsements.

3. **To view the profile page of one of these influencers, select his avatar.**

To view your +K within your Notifications list

1. **Make sure you are logged in to Klout.com by signing in with Twitter or Facebook.**

2. **Click the icon with three lines in a row that resembles notebook paper (see Figure 7-20).**

   This icon is next to your name and avatar in the top-right side of the screen.

Figure 7-20: Klout Notifications tab.

A drop-down menu appears with your notifications. Here you see who recently gave you +K and in which topic.

3. **If you wish to publicly share this information via Twitter or Facebook, click a notification within this list and choose a sharing option (shown in Figure 7-21).**

Figure 7-21: Thank influencers for their endorsement via Twitter or Facebook.

Chapter 8

Enjoying Klout Perks

- -

- -

*F*or many influencers, qualifying for Klout Perks is one of the most enjoyable features of the website. Klout Perks are free products or discounts on goods or services from a wide variety of brands. Perks are awarded based on a number of criteria (including geographic location and topics of influence) to benefit brands and influencers alike. Rewarding influencers for their hard work is a great way to get people talking about a new product or service.

Brands partner with Klout to get their new products in front of potential consumers, and many influencers appreciate being among the first to try something new. As a result, Klout benefits from increased visibility, and everyone wins.

I like to think of Klout Perks in the same way as reward bucks at my local grocery store. They are nice little benefits when you take advantage of them. Although it may not directly impact your overall Klout Score, claiming a Perk is a fun way of interacting with the site and often, your followers.

In this chapter, you find out how to locate and claim your Perks, share information about Perks with your followers, and properly disclose products and services on your social sharing sites. Klout Perks are an ever-changing benefit for online influencers. I wish you the best of luck in claiming and using your free goodies!

Pointing to Perks

Finding your Perks on the Klout website (see Figure 8-1) is a pretty simple process. Because eligibility is based on your Klout Score, geographic location, and topics of influence, you never know what may pop up.

Perks

Figure 8-1: Klout Perks menu.

To locate your Perks menu, simply do the following:

1. **Log in to Klout by pointing your browser to** `www.klout.com` **and signing in with either Facebook or Twitter.**

2. **Select Perks from the navigation bar in the upper right corner of the screen.**

3. **View Perks in the drop-down list that appears.**

Some Perks are better than others, and available Perks change from time to time — so checking out your Perks menu regularly is a good idea. Doing so helps make sure that you don't miss out on a Perk you want to grab.

Searching for Perks

Klout lists all Perks-related information in your Perks notification menu located to the left of your name and avatar in the upper-right corner of the screen. The Perks menu lists Perks for which you are eligible, as shown in Figure 8-2, as well as opportunities to provide feedback on Perks you've already claimed. Perks can offer a range of items — from free food to beauty products. You may also see discount codes for online services like photo books and business cards.

Figure 8-2: A list of Perks in the notification menu.

Perks come in all shapes and sizes. Some categories on the Klout website include these:

- ✔ **Featured:** These are current Perks specifically promoted by Klout.

- ✔ **Entertainment:** This category includes items related to television shows or tickets to movies and theme parks.

- ✔ **Experiences:** Much like entertainment, this category typically includes opportunities to attend live events.

- ✔ **Food and Beverage:** You can receive discounts on products or free samples mailed to your home through this category.

✔ **Retail:** This category offers free samples or full-size products and discounts for online retailers.

✔ **Sports:** Check out items like sports-related discounts and freebies ranging from fantasy football points to protein shakes and magazine subscriptions.

✔ **Technology:** Get the latest on new apps, websites, and products for technology lovers.

✔ **Klout for Good:** You can claim cause-oriented Perks that allow you to give back. Prior campaigns include The American Heart Association.

For the purposes of this chapter, I focus on the goods and services categories. I discuss the Klout for Good category in detail in Chapter 9.

Your Perks notifications menu includes the most recent fifteen notifications, whether you became eligible for a Perk or a brand requested feedback based on a Perk you claimed.

Determining your eligibility for Perks

When you're eligible for a Perk, it appears in your notifications menu (see Figure 8-3). From there, if you wish to claim the Perk, simply click it and follow the instructions that I describe in this chapter. A Perk doesn't appear if you aren't eligible to claim it. However, some Perks are very popular or have a short supply. If you don't claim a Perk right away, you may see a message saying that the Perk is full or that you have the option to be added to a wait list.

Eligibility for Perks is determined by a number of different criteria such as age, geographic location, topics of influence, Klout Score, and parenting status. Different brands reach out to different demographics for different reasons, so you will likely see a variety of offers over time.

I was recently selected for a Perk from Starbucks. The criteria for this Perk (shown in Figure 8-4) were influencers who live in the United States with a Klout Score above 40 and a coffee-related category among their topics of influence. I often chat with friends about coffee, so Klout was right to offer me this Perk. I couldn't claim that Perk fast enough!

When you are selected for a perk, you will see the criteria for selection when you go through the claiming process as I describe in this chapter.

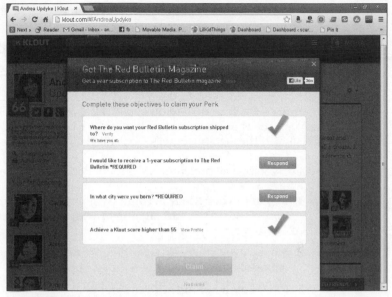

Figure 8-3: Claim your Perk.

Figure 8-4: I'm in!

Like many automated online programs, the system doesn't always get it right. You may be matched with a brand that's not a fit for you, or you may be passed over for what seems like the perfect opportunity. Klout is continually improving this process to make the experience better for everyone.

You aren't required to accept a Perk that you're eligible for.

Getting e-mail notification for Perks

If you aren't in the habit of visiting Klout on a regular basis, you can create an e-mail alert for Perks. When you are eligible for a Perk, Klout will e-mail you and let you know. However, although I have received e-mails on occasion alerting me to current Perks, some have slipped through the cracks, so I still visit Klout regularly.

To set up your e-mail preferences for Klout Perks, follow these steps:

1. **Log in to your Klout account by pointing your browser to** www.klout.com **and signing in with either Facebook or Twitter.**

2. **Mouse over your name in the upper-right corner and choose Settings from the list that appears.**

3. **Click Email Settings in the sidebar.**

4. **Select your e-mail preferences. To receive e-mail notifications, select the check box next to the Klout Perks heading at the bottom of the page (see Figure 8-5). If you don't wish to receive e-mail notifications, leave the box deselected.**

5. **Click the Save Settings button.**

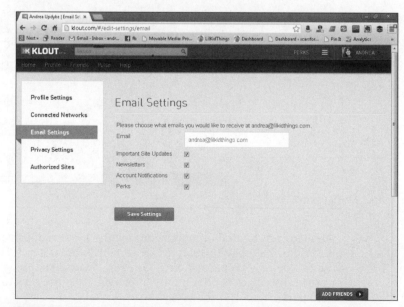

Figure 8-5: Perks e-mail settings.

Grabbing the Goodies

I still get a little thrill when I see that I'm eligible for a Klout Perk. In the past, I've snapped up free nail polish, Starbucks coffee, t-shirts, and more. I often forget that I have claimed something until it arrives in my mailbox, which doubles the fun! Here's how you, too, can enjoy Perks.

Claiming your Perks

Congratulations! When you're eligible for a Klout Perk, all you need to do is claim it and you're on your way to enjoying a special treat.

If you see a Klout Perk you want, claim it right away! Perks are limited and awarded on a first-come, first-served basis. If the Perk is full, you may be allowed to join a waitlist.

To claim your Perk, follow these easy steps:

1. **Log in to your Klout account by pointing your browser to** www.klout.com **and signing in with either Facebook or Twitter.**

2. **If you have a Perk, your notifications menu will show a number over the word** *Perks*. **Click Perks to open the menu.**

3. **If you wish to claim your Perk, select it from the menu.**

   A pop-up appears, with instructions to claim your perk. Here, you can read a little more about the offer and decide if you want to claim it.

4. **To claim the Perk, click the orange Get Started button.**

   A window opens with further instructions for how to claim this Perk and sometimes includes some of the criteria used to award you this Perk (shown in Figure 8-6).

5. **Verify or enter your address in the fields provided and click Claim to complete the process.**

If you would like to save time when claiming Perks in the future, be sure to enter your contact information in your Profile settings page, as shown in Figure 8-7. By doing so, Klout stores your information so the next time you claim a Perk, you're asked only to verify your mailing information.

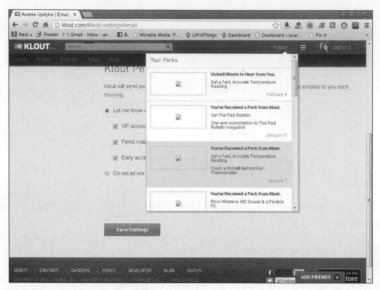

Figure 8-6: Claim Your Perk!

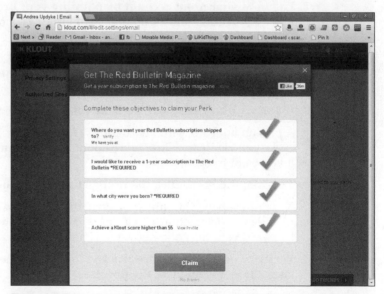

Figure 8-7: Enter the requested information to claim your Perk.

If your Perk is related to an online benefit, you may be given a code or directed to the retailer's website to claim your Perk (as shown in Figure 8-8). If you don't want to do it right away, this information is available to you anytime you log in to Klout. See the next section for info on how to do that.

Figure 8-8: Instructions for claiming an online Perk.

Using your online Perk

To use a Perk for an online service, you are either given a code or directed to the brand website to complete your offer. If you receive a code, simply redeem it according to the brand-specific instructions before the expiration date.

In the case of a special offer, go to the website by clicking the link provided on Klout.com to be sure the brand recognizes you as the recipient of a Perk and credits you with the deal.

If you want to claim a Perk but aren't yet ready to use it, don't worry! Your information is saved in Klout. To find it, click on the Perk in your Perks menu. When you click it, your Perk information and how to claim it appears.

Sharing your Perk

After you claim your Perk, you have the option to tell your friends and followers about the Perk you claimed. If they're eligible, they will also be able to take advantage of the offer. However, social sharing is not a requirement to be able to claim a Perk. If you don't want to share this information, feel free to click Skip or simply close the sharing dialog box pictured in Figure 8-9.

Figure 8-9: Tell friends and followers about a Perk you've claimed.

Via the sharing dialog that appears after you've claimed your Perk, you can tell followers and friends on Twitter or Facebook about the Perk you're getting. Click either the Twitter or Facebook buttons for a prewritten status update and share. You may use this update as-is or personalize the message in your own voice.

If you are not logged in to your social networks, you need to enter your username and password before updating your status.

Leaving feedback about your Perk

Opening your mailbox to find a neatly wrapped package from Klout is a lot of fun. After you've had a chance to try out your Perk, you may want to assign a rating and leave some feedback about the Perk you received. Klout will request your feedback a few weeks after you claim a Perk, as shown in Figure 8-10. Your feedback not only helps brands understand their consumer better, but also lets Klout know what kind of Perks are creating the best buzz.

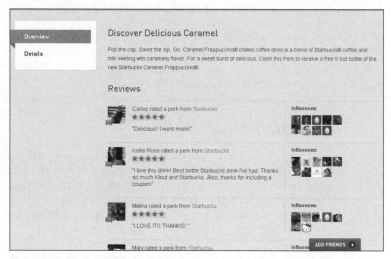

Figure 8-10: Klout request for feedback.

Leaving feedback is totally voluntary, but there have been times when I really appreciated an item and wanted to make sure I left feedback. For instance, I was recently awarded the Perk of 50 free business cards from Moo.com. Using my Klout Perk was easy and I walked away with the most beautiful business cards

I have ever seen. I rated my experience highly and left positive feedback because I was very satisfied. I would love to see more Perks from Moo.

You can leave feedback in the form of a star rating (from one to five stars, as shown previously in Figure 8-10) and/or by leaving a comment in the Reviews section of the page. Follow these steps:

1. **Log in to your Klout account by pointing your browser to** www.klout.com **and signing in with either Facebook or Twitter.**

2. **Navigate to your Perks menu in the upper right corner of your screen and select a feedback request.**

    A pop up window appears.

3. **Provide the requested information to review your perk.**

    Depending on the perk, your review options vary. Potential rating tools are listed at the end of these instructions.

4. **Click Submit to complete your review.**

    A pop-up box appears that gives you the option to share this Perk.

5. **You may share at this time or click Continue to skip this step.**

    You return to the original review page showing a check mark next to the statement *Review this Perk*. Your feedback is posted publicly in the feedback section for the Perk. To read more reviews, select the View Feedback link in this window.

6. **Close this box by clicking the** *x* **in the upper-right corner of the pop-up.**

    Some ways to rate a Perk are as follows:

    - *Rate it.* Choose the number of stars (from one to five) that you want to award to this Perk by hovering over each star until it turns orange and click.

    - *Review it.* Leave written feedback in your own words about this Perk.

    - *Add a picture.* Upload a picture of your Perk if you wish by clicking the Add a Picture button and uploading it from your hard drive.

Disclosing Your Perks

Blogging or social sharing about any Klout Perks you receive is absolutely voluntary. In fact, you could potentially claim Perks indefinitely without ever mentioning it online. However, if you do choose to blog about your Perk online or via social networks (like Facebook and Twitter), it's important to disclose that you received it as a Perk from Klout. Here are some recommendations on how to do that.

Posting a disclosure on your blog

If you choose to feature a product on your blog or website that you received as a Klout Perk, it's important to disclose this information to your readers so you are in compliance with the Federal Trade Commission. Your disclosure doesn't need to be complicated; it just needs to be present.

According to the Federal Trade Commission (FTC),

> . . . "material connections" (sometimes payments or free products) between advertisers and endorsers – connections that consumers would not expect – must be disclosed. These examples address what constitutes an endorsement when the message is conveyed by bloggers or other "word-of-mouth" marketers. The revised Guides specify that while decisions will be reached on a case-by-case basis, the post of a blogger who receives cash or in-kind payment to review a product is considered an endorsement. . .

For the full article regarding FTC requirements, point your browser to www.ftc.gov/opa/2009/10/endortest.shtm.

A sample blog disclosure might look something like the one on my personal blog post (and shown in Figure 8-11). When I reviewed a product for CSN Stores, I added this disclaimer at the end of the post:

> Disclosure: I was provided with a gift certificate from CSN store to do a review.

If you blog about a Perk you receive on Klout, adding this disclaimer to the end of the post should suffice:

> Disclosure: I received the above product for free (or a discount) via Klout. All opinions are my own.

Disclosure

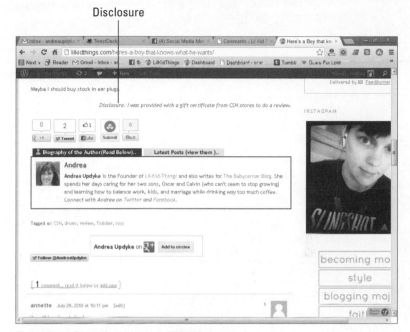

Figure 8-11: Blog disclosure on lilkidthings.com.

Disclosing Perks via social networks

If you post about a claimed Perk via one of your social networks, it is good practice to disclose it there as well. You can do this by thanking Klout and the company for the free product or discount, or simply mentioning that you got it for free. Of course, you don't have to mention it at all. But if you do, honesty is always the best policy.

For example, you might use a hashtag symbol (#) for a Twitter disclosure, as suggested by the FTC here:

> A hashtag like "#paid ad" uses only 8 characters. Shorter hashtags – like "#paid" and "#ad" – also might be effective.

You can find the full article here:

```
http://business.ftc.gov/documents/bus71-ftcs-
revised-endorsement-guideswhat-people-are-asking
```

Using a disclosure should not be a deterrent to sharing your opinion about a product. In fact, being honest and upfront with your community will only benefit your influence in the long run.

Chapter 9

Doing Good through Klout

● ●

In This Chapter

▶ Finding ways to help others

▶ Using your influence for good

▶ Realizing the benefits of social good

● ●

Klout is increasingly becoming a way to measure social influence whether you're using the site as a businessperson, blogger, entertainer, or scholar. It's fun to watch the different ways you can increase your influence. Even better is using that influence to help others. With Klout for Good, millions of people have been educated about a wide range of topics.

Klout for Good is a social program in which influencers can share programs and initiatives that support charity organizations via tweets and Facebook updates. Klout believes that by donating your influence, you can help raise awareness and support for people in need. And who knows? You may even learn a thing or two!

Contributing to Social Programs

Klout has helped a number of different social programs by offering influencers the chance to share information via their social networks (Twitter and Facebook). Klout introduces a new social campaign monthly, and influencers can use the social sharing buttons to share it with their followers.

Tweets and Facebook shares are built in to each campaign to make sharing easy. Details about each program and a link back to the charity page on the Klout website are included (as shown in Figure 9-1).

Figure 9-1: A Klout for Good tweet.

Finding out about Klout for Good causes

The amount of need in the world is truly overwhelming, and it's easy to feel small and helpless when facing such need. The Klout approach is appealing due to its simplicity and integration with social media. I've become more aware by learning about the various charities Klout has worked with and I've found some that I want to support because of those connections. Knowing about the need is the first step in helping to fix it.

To locate programs through Klout for Good and share via Facebook or Twitter, simply follow these instructions:

1. **Point your browser to** www.klout.com/s/forgood.

   The most recent campaign is highlighted at the top of the page (shown in Figure 9-2).

2. **Click the gold Learn More button to open the campaign page.**

3. **Read about the campaign and follow the links to the charity website to get more details or donate time or money.**

Figure 9-2: Klout for Good home page.

4. **Raise awareness in your own social circles by either tweeting or sharing a Facebook status about the campaign, as described in the next section.**

The most recent campaign is shown at the top of the Klout for Good page, but you'll find a few more campaigns as you scroll down the page. Campaigns are listed in chronological order with the most recent month's campaign at the top.

Donate your influence by sharing Klout for Good campaigns on Facebook and Twitter at any time. There is never a shortage of need!

Donating influence

You can donate your social influence via Klout for Good in a few ways. Sharing information through your social networks (Twitter and Facebook) is certainly the easiest and quickest way to help. However, you can also find opportunities to donate time and money when you visit the charity website.

In December 2012, Klout partnered with Operation: Social Santa to collect and distribute toys for underprivileged children. Through this program, influencers had the opportunity to create awareness, donate toys, and even head up collection teams in their city. How much or how little you give is up to you, and every little bit counts.

Your influence matters! It isn't the quantity of followers you have on your social networks, but the quality of interactions that really makes a difference. When you leverage your influence to provide valuable information about ways your followers can give back or learn about what's important to you, you contribute a rich and valuable social dialog. And if you can help someone in the process, that's even better!

To donate your influence via Twitter, follow these steps:

1. **Make sure you are logged in to Klout.com by signing in with your Twitter or Facebook account in the upper-right corner of Klout.com.**

2. **Visit** `www.klout.com/s/forgood` **and locate the campaign you wish to share.**

3. **Select the campaign by clicking the photo.**

4. **Click the Twitter social share button.**

   A pop-up box appears with a pre-written message included (see Figure 9-3).

Figure 9-3: Klout for Good tweet.

5. **Edit the text of your tweet here or leave it as is.**

6. **When you have the message you want to share, click Tweet.**

   Your tweet now appears in your Twitter feed.

You can also share social good programs from Klout via your Facebook Timeline. Klout makes it easy to share with the embedded social share button.

To donate your influence via Facebook, follow these steps:

1. **Make sure you are logged in to Klout.com by signing in with your Twitter or Facebook account in the upper-right corner of Klout.com.**

2. **Point your browser to** www.klout.com/s/forgood **and scroll down the page until you see the campaign you want to share.**

3. **Select the campaign by clicking the photo.**

4. **Share with your Facebook friends or fans by clicking the Facebook social share button.**

   A pop-up box appears (as shown in Figure 9-4).

Figure 9-4: Create a Klout for Good Facebook post.

5. **To create your post, add a message in the text box or simply post the link.**

6. **Complete your post by clicking the blue Share button.**

   Your Facebook post is shared to your Facebook Timeline and appears in your friends' News Feeds.

You don't have to be limited by the social share buttons on Klout! To share a Klout for Good campaign on other social networks not represented by the social share buttons, simply copy the link associated with the campaign you wish to promote and paste it into the status box in whatever social network you prefer (such as Google+ or LinkedIn). Feel free to add your own message along with the link to get people interested!

Reviewing Successful Campaigns

In 2012, Klout partnered with some amazing organizations to create campaigns that helped raise awareness about some pretty significant issues around the world. By partnering with these organizations and individual influencers, millions of people have been educated about topics from the need for clean water in Africa to poverty in San Francisco to AIDS prevention around the world.

Through these campaigns, influencers have used social media to raise money, donate toys, and educate and provide life-giving sustenance to countless people in need. You can follow the Klout for Good journey and learn more about Klout for Good by visiting the Klout corporate blog at `http://corp.klout.com/blog/category/klout-for-good` (shown in Figure 9-5).

Figure 9-5: Klout for Good blog category.

Klout believes that no influence is too small, which is why each campaign provides several ways to contribute. It's okay if you can't always donate money. Maybe you can donate your time, or a toy, or use your voice to spread the word. No matter how you help, it's always appreciated by the people who need it.

Successful campaigns through Klout for Good include charity: water, the World Wildlife Fund, and The San Francisco Food Bank and Marin Food Bank, among others. Through these programs, influencers and Klout employees learn about needs, raise awareness in others, and donate their resources to give back. And give back, they do!

charity: water

Klout ran two different campaigns for charity: water in 2012 — one in the spring and one in the fall. This important cause is seeking to provide clean drinking water to thousands of families in Rwanda.

With its first campaign in March 2012, Klout asked influencers to donate their birthdays to charity: water (shown in Figure 9-6). By donating their birthdays, influencers pledged to forgo personal birthday gifts and instead gave that money to the effort of providing clean drinking water to people who need it in Rwanda. Those who were not able to donate financially donated their influence by tweeting and sharing via Facebook.

Figure 9-6: March 2012 charity: water campaign.

A few months later, in September 2012, Klout for Good was at it again. In this campaign (shown in Figure 9-7), Klout for Good encouraged influencers to help charity: water meet its goal of raising $1.7 million and provide clean drinking water to almost 26,000 people in two sectors of the Rulindo district in Rwanda.

Figure 9-7: charity: water September goal met!

Not only did the people at charity: water meet their goal, they exceeded it and continued to raise money through the end of the year to give many more families in Rwanda the vital resource of clean water.

To learn more about charity: water, visit its webpage at www. charitywater.org. It's not too late to donate your birthday or support this cause!

World Wildlife Fund

Another organization that benefitted from partnering with Klout for Good is the World Wildlife Fund (WWF). During the month of April 2012, Klout encouraged influencers to help raise awareness for Arctic preservation (see Figure 9-8).

Influencers were encouraged to contribute by sharing links in their social networks, donating money, learning how to reduce waste in their personal lives, or using one of the beautiful WWF Facebook Timeline cover images on their Facebook profiles and Pages (shown in Figure 9-9).

Figure 9-8: Klout for Good partners with the World Wildlife Fund.

Figure 9-9: Facebook Timeline photos provided by the World Wildlife Fund.

To learn more about the World Wildlife Fund and support this cause, check out its website at `http://worldwildlife.org`.

San Francisco and Marin Food Banks

Although there are looming issues and people in need all over the world, there is also plenty of need right here at home. Klout recognized this when it decided to partner with the San Francisco and Marin Food Banks in November 2012 (see Figure 9-10).

Figure 9-10: Give back with Klout for Good to San Francisco and Marin Food Banks.

By partnering with these food banks, Klout raised awareness for hunger and poverty issues in America and reminded influencers of ways to give back to their own communities. With 1 in 4 families in San Francisco in need of food assistance, any gift of time or money won't go to waste.

Klout led by example when a team of Klout employees showed up to volunteer at the food bank. By the end of the day, volunteers sorted through almost 15,000 pounds of food to be distributed to families in need (see Figure 9-11).

You can help the San Francisco and Marin communities and learn more by visiting their website at www.sffoodbank.org. Or locate a food bank near you by visiting http://feedingamerica.org.

Figure 9-11: Klout employees volunteer at San Francisco and Marin Food Banks.

Operation: Social Santa

To end the year with a smile, Klout gave influencers the chance to be Santa by connecting them with a project called Operation: Social Santa, which can be found at www.operationsocial santa.com (shown in Figure 9-12).

Through this program across the U.S., volunteers hosted holiday parties to collect toys to be distributed to children in need. The program, started in 2010, has donated thousands of toys to under-privileged children right here in America.

Through the Klout for Good partnership (shown in Figure 9-13), influencers raised awareness through their social networks by sharing links, using the Twitter hashtag #socialsanta, donating toys, and volunteering to host local events.

Figure 9-12: Operation: Social Santa website.

Figure 9-13: Klout for Good partners with Operation: Social Santa to provide toys for kids in need.

Getting Involved with Klout for Good

To partner with Klout on a campaign for good or to learn other ways you can get involved, e-mail Klout using the address good@ klout.com.

Klout for Good campaigns are updated on a monthly basis. Don't forget to check back each month to find out how you can leverage your influence for social good!

Chapter 10

Managing Visibility in Klout

· ·

In This Chapter

▶ Learning to navigate your privacy settings

▶ Removing Klout Moments from your profile page

▶ Opting out of Klout.com

· ·

*W*hen you think about Internet privacy, it may seem a little (or a lot) overwhelming. Most of your online activity is public in some way, from the comments you make on blog posts to the pictures and status updates you share across the various social media networks. Learning the various privacy options on each website you use can be daunting, but that doesn't mean it's impossible.

Klout compares its method with other analytics services (such as Google Analytics) that extract information from public resources to make certain calculations, including website traffic. It may seem strange that your information can be mined in this way, but it can and does happen regularly. You do have options, however. If you decide using Klout is not for you, or you wish to customize the information it uses, you have the right to do so at any time by reviewing your privacy settings.

Managing Privacy Concerns

Klout offers a few ways to customize the way people see information when they view your profile. You can remove specific Moments that appear, completely opt out of showing Moments at all, or block certain users. These options are available to you on the Privacy Settings page.

A good rule of thumb to remember when discussing Internet privacy is that the Internet itself is a public space and even in situations that seem private, remember not to share anything you don't want the world to see. I don't mean to scare you, but I'm simply reminding you that what you put out into the world via the Internet is going to stay out there for a very long time.

When Klout uses data to determine a Score, it's using only public data. Klout is a public service that uses public information found on the Internet to calculate influence. I like to think of it as a big spreadsheet with all of my tweets, status updates, and shares laid out on one side of the page and all of the actions my followers took in response on the other. None of the information is private, but it's all in one place so it can be measured.

In general, the information you share as a social media user is out there in the world for anyone to see, barring specific privacy settings. So when Klout calculates your Score, this data is what it's mining from your public online activity.

Reviewing privacy settings

Klout has some built-in restrictions for you already in place. For instance, although you can look at your profile and see your highlights of both private and public information, when someone else looks at your profile, she sees information based on which networks she already connects with you.

For example, if one of your highlighted Moments is a Facebook status that was intended for only your Facebook friends, only those friends see that Moment when viewing your Klout profile. You can see who is able to view your post by looking at the icon next to the timestamp on your post. If the icon is a globe, the post is public.

Figure 10-1 shows one of my Facebook Moments. You can see that the icon is the Facebook privacy symbol that means friends only. In Klout, that means only my Facebook friends are able to see this Moment on my profile.

If a stranger views your profile, a friends-only post simply won't appear. The same rule applies to other social networks in which you might have private posts (such as restricted Twitter or Instagram accounts).

To view your privacy settings in Klout, follow these steps:

1. **Log in to Klout.com by connecting via your Twitter or Facebook account in the upper-right corner of the screen.**

2. **Click your name in the upper-right corner and select Settings from the drop-down menu that appears.**

3. **Choose Privacy Settings from the list of options on the left side of your screen (shown in Figure 10-2).**

From this screen, you can read the entire Klout privacy policy by following the link at the top of the page. You can also adjust your Klout moments and view any users you have blocked.

Friends

Figure 10-1: Only Facebook friends see this Moment.

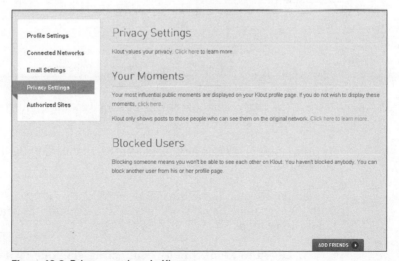

Figure 10-2: Privacy settings in Klout.

To read Klout's entire privacy policy, you can do so by visiting this webpage, `http://klout.com/#/corp/your_privacy`.

Removing Moments from your profile

You can also remove Moments from your profile completely and block specific users from seeing your profile information.

Your most influential public Moments appear on your profile page unless you indicate otherwise. You can either remove all Moments from your profile page or one at a time.

To remove all Moments from appearing on your Klout profile page

1. **Log in to Klout.com by connecting via your Twitter or Facebook account in the upper-right corner of the screen.**

2. **Click your name in the upper-right corner and select Settings from the drop-down menu that appears.**

3. **Open your Privacy Settings page by choosing Privacy Settings from the list of options on the left side of your screen.**

4. **Scroll down to the Your Moments section and select the Click Here link after the text, *If you do not wish to display these moments,* (shown in Figure 10-3).**

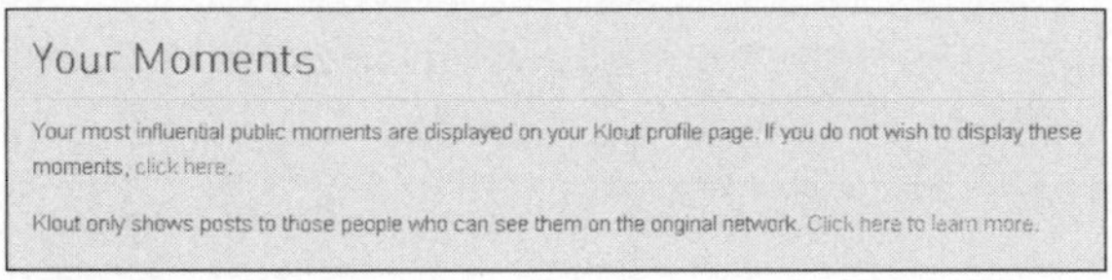

Your Moments

Your most influential public moments are displayed on your Klout profile page. If you do not wish to display these moments, click here.

Klout only shows posts to those people who can see them on the original network. Click here to learn more.

Figure 10-3: Remove all Klout Moments from your profile page.

The page refreshes and your social media highlights no longer appear on your Klout profile page.

If you wish to undo this action, select the Display My Public Moments link.

To remove specific Moments from your Klout profile page (but not from the social media network in which it originally appeared), follow these steps:

1. **Log in to Klout.com by connecting via your Twitter or Facebook account in the upper-right corner of the screen.**

2. **Click Profile in the top-left side of the navigation bar.**

   Your highlighted Moments are listed in the main column of your profile page.

3. **Mouse over the Moment you wish to delete and click the *x* in the upper-right corner of the text box (shown in Figure 10-4).**

   Your moment no longer appears in Klout.

Figure 10-4: Delete a highlighted Moment from your profile page.

Blocking users

Occasionally, you may have the need to block an influencer. When you block an influencer in Klout, he or she can't view your profile. Instead, when the blocked user clicks your name, a screen appears saying, "This page does not exist," as shown in Figure 10-5. Likewise when you block another influencer, you will no longer be able to view his or her profile and will see the same error message.

Figure 10-5: This is what a blocked user sees.

If you decide to block someone, the process is simple:

1. **Search for the influencer using the search bar at the top of your screen.**

   A page opens with a list of users.

2. **Select the user you wish to block.**

3. **Scroll down until you see the words Block and then the name of the user (for example, Block Andrea Updyke) located below topics of influence in the left sidebar.**

   Note: The font is a lighter color than the rest of the text on the page (see Figure 10-6).

4. **Click Block *User*.**

   A pop-up confirmation appears (shown in Figure 10-7).

5. **If you wish to block this influencer, click Okay.**

   If you decide not to block him, simply click No Thanks, or close the pop-up using the *x* in the top-right corner of the box.

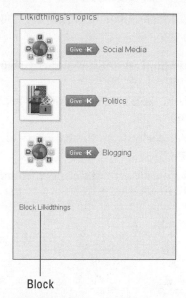

Block

Figure 10-6: Block this user.

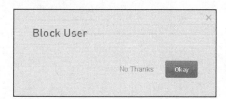

Figure 10-7: Confirmation to block a user in Klout.

Disconnecting Social Networks

You have the option of connecting many (if not all) of your social networks to Klout, and the service is adding more all of the time. The benefit of adding networks is that you have a more accurate Klout Score. Klout is continuously trying to make its algorithm more accurate and add data from an increasing number of sources. If you use most of your networks publicly, adding them to Klout makes sense. (I discuss connecting networks in Chapter 7.) You can also remove them at any time.

If you decide that you want to disconnect a network from Klout, it's a very straightforward process.

1. **Make sure you are logged in to Klout.com by signing in in the upper-right corner of the screen.**

2. **Mouse over your name and select Settings from the drop-down menu that appears.**

3. **Select Connected Networks from the list of options on the left side of your screen.**

4. **Locate the network you wish to disconnect from Klout and click the Unlink link (shown in Figure 10-8).**

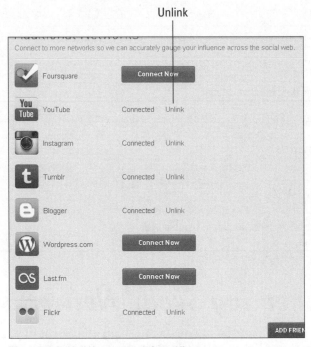

Unlink

Figure 10-8: Unlink a network from Klout.

The page refreshes and next to the network, you see the Connect Now button next to the network icon. This means that particular network is no longer connected.

Deleting Your Account

If you decide that you no longer wish to participate in Klout, you can opt out completely by visiting the opt-out page on Klout.com.

You can access this page by entering the following URL into your address bar in your Internet browser, `http://klout.com/#/edit-settings/optout`.

Because Klout uses public information pulled from the Internet, it may already have some data stored for you even if you have not signed up for Klout. Whether or not you have a Klout account, you can opt out of this data collection.

If you already have a Klout account and you want to opt out of Klout.com, do the following:

1. **Make sure you are logged in to Klout.**

2. **Point your browser to the Opting Out of Klout page located at** `http://klout.com/#/edit-settings/optout`.

3. **Scroll to the bottom of the page and click the Continue Opting-Out link.**

   A new page opens, as shown in Figure 10-9.

4. **Provide Klout with your reason for opting out and type your name in the "signature" box provided.**

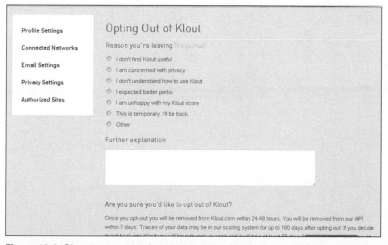

Figure 10-9: Give a reason and type your name in the box provided to opt out of Klout.

5. **Click Submit to complete the opting-out process.**

If you've never signed up for Klout and wish to have your public profile removed from the website, the process is slightly different.

1. **Point your browser to** `http://klout.com/corp/optout` **and scroll to the bottom of the page.**

   You will need to verify that you are the owner of the Klout account in question by allowing Klout to connect with either your Twitter or Facebook account.

2. **Select the account to use and click OK or Allow to verify your identity.**

   A new page opens.

3. **Provide Klout with your reason for opting out and type your name in the "signature" box provided.**

4. **Click Submit to complete the opting out process.**

 Because of the nature of information on the Internet, it may take some time for your ties with Klout to disappear. Klout states that accounts take about 24 to 48 hours to be disconnected, but traces of Klout Scores and data can take up to 180 days to completely flush out of its data scoring system.

After you are removed from the Klout system, you can always reconnect later. Just remember that after Klout stops collecting your data, it can take up to 90 days to gather enough new data to provide an accurate Score.

Chapter 11

Exploring Mobile Options for Android Users

*A*t the time of writing this book, Klout has not yet developed an official app for Android users. According to their FAQ, the folks at Klout are working on one. But in the meantime, Klout users who operate on Android mobile devices still have a few options.

In this chapter, I review three unofficial apps available to Android users.

- ✔ **Klout for Android:** Connect to this app using your Twitter name. You have the ability to share your Score via Twitter and Facebook as well as view your top five topics and fellow influencers.

- ✔ **Klout Droid:** Developed by Pete Yagmin, this app provides a simple screenshot of your Score and a few influencers. You also have the ability to tweet your Score via the app.

- ✔ **Klout Widget (Beta):** This widget is about as simple as it gets. After you configure it properly, it simply shows your Klout Score on the home screen of your Android device.

Until Klout develops an official app, these options allow you to keep tabs on your Klout Score using your Android device. Whether you simply want to monitor your Score or search for other Klout users, these simple apps allow you to accomplish your goals.

If you wish to dig deeper into your options in Klout, you can always log in to the full site using a browser on your Android device. Doing so allows you to use all of the features Klout has to offer.

Looking for Android Apps

To search for Android apps, open the Google Play store on your device and type **Klout** into the search bar (shown in Figure 11-1).

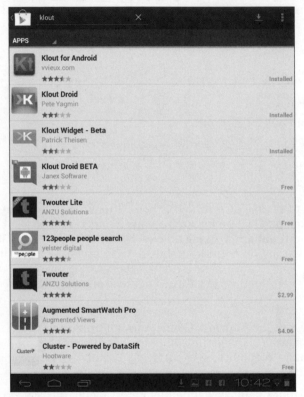

Figure 11-1: Search for apps in the Google Play store.

Tap an app to read its description and reviews. After you find the app you want to install, tap the Install button to begin the installation to your Android device. Then you can begin to view and configure your app as discussed in the sections that follow.

Using Klout for Android

The Klout for Android app was created by vvieux.com and is the most comprehensive of the three apps that I review in this chapter. With this app, you can view your current Klout Score and share it via Twitter and Facebook, and view your top five topics and ten of your fellow influencers.

To begin, install the Klout for Android app via the Google Play store. After you install the app, configuration is easy.

1. **Open Klout for Android by tapping the icon on your home screen.**

   A screen appears prompting you to enter a Twitter name (as shown in Figure 11-2).

Figure 11-2: Klout for Android login screen.

2. **Type in your Twitter name, without the @ symbol in front of it, and tap the View button.**

   A limited version of your profile appears.

Your profile screen (mine is shown in Figure 11-3) contains quite a bit of information for a limited app. Starting at the top of the page, you can view your Klout Score as well as the following:

✔ **Amplification details:** This is an older Klout metric that scores how your messages are carried throughout your social networks.

✔ **True reach:** This shows the number of people you communicate with via your social networks.

✔ **Network Score:** This measures the average Score of the influencers you connect with.

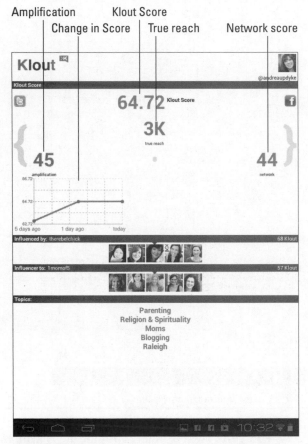

Figure 11-3: Klout Score information within the Klout for Android App.

✔ **Change in Score:** At the bottom of your Score section, a chart displaying the change in your Score over the past five days appears. This helpful visual gives you an at-a-glance idea of the general growth or decline of your Klout Score.

The next section within this app is an interactive list of the top five influencers you're influenced by followed by the top five people you influence (shown earlier in Figure 11-3). Using your finger to slide the icons to the left or right, you can view each influencer's name and Klout Score. Finally, you can click each person's photo icon to go to his profile screen, where you can view his Score, influencers, and topics.

Finally, your profile screen has a list of the top five topics in which Klout believes you to be influential. At this time the list is not interactive, and you cannot use it to endorse fellow influencers; it's purely informational.

Sharing your Klout Score via Twitter and Facebook is easy with the Klout for Android app. To do so, simply tap on the Twitter or Facebook icons on the top left and right of the screen. This opens a new window with a status update for you to share. As always, make sure you are logged in to your social networks to use this feature.

Reviewing Klout Droid

Developed by Pete Yagmin, this is another one-screen app that allows you to view basic Klout updates using your Android device. See the app's detail screen in the Google Play store in Figure 11-4.

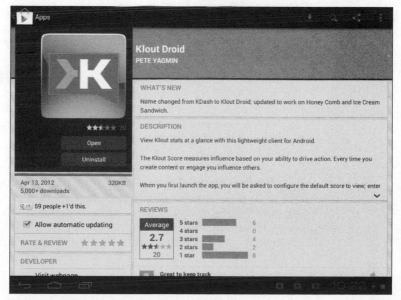

Figure 11-4: Klout Droid app for Android devices.

Getting started is easy after you download and install the app via the Google Play store. As with Klout for Android, you can use only your Twitter account to log in to this app.

Don't forget to leave off the @ symbol when logging in to the Klout Droid app! You only need to type your Twitter name.

A profile screen (shown in Figure 11-5) appears after you're logged in to Klout Droid. On this screen, you see the following features:

✔ **Your Klout Score:** The Klout Droid software connects with Klout to update your score so the most current score is displayed when you view your app.

✔ **A social sharing button for Twitter only:** You may share your Score using the Twitter sharing button. At this time, Twitter is the only social network you can share with via the Klout Droid app.

✔ **Your network Score details:** Like Klout for Android, the Klout Droid app allows you to review certain details about your Score, including the average Score of your network, true reach, and amplification probability.

✔ **The top five people you influence:** View the names and Klout Scores of the top five people you influence. Names are also hyperlinked so you can click an influencer and view her profile.

✔ **The top five people you are influenced by:** View another five names, including the people who most influence you, along with their Klout Scores. Follow their links to view each influencer's profile.

✔ **A search box to find other influencers by Twitter name:** To view the Klout Score of an influencer who does not appear in your profile, simply enter the person's Twitter name in the search field and tap the View Klout button. Remember to leave out the @ symbol when you enter an influencer's name.

In the upper-right corner of your profile screen in Klout Droid, a gear icon takes you to the Configuration page (shown in Figure 11-6). By tapping this gear, you can change the default profile that appears each time you open the app. This may be useful if you manage more than one Klout account that you wish to monitor on your Android device.

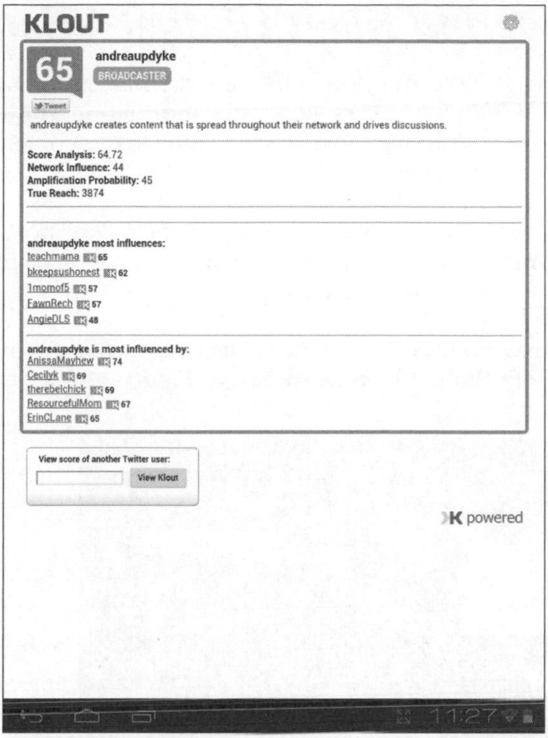

Figure 11-5: Klout Droid profile screen.

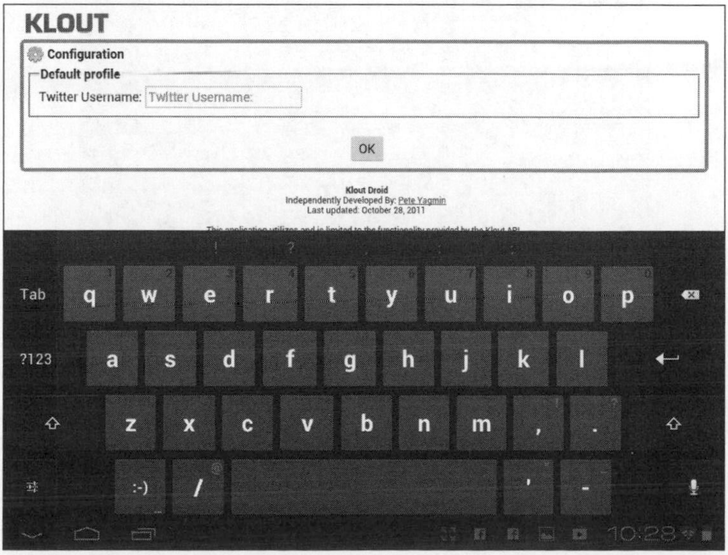

Figure 11-6: Klout Droid Configuration page.

Discovering Klout Widget - Beta

Klout Widget - Beta, developed by Patrick Theisen, is a widget, not an app, and therefore offers very little information. However, if you wish to view your Klout Score on the home screen of your Android device, this widget gets it done.

To install your Klout Widget, go to the Google Play store and download it just like you would an app. To add the Klout Widget to your home screen after it's installed, follow these steps:

1. **Open your collection of widgets and find the orange Klout Widget icon as shown in Figure 11-7.**

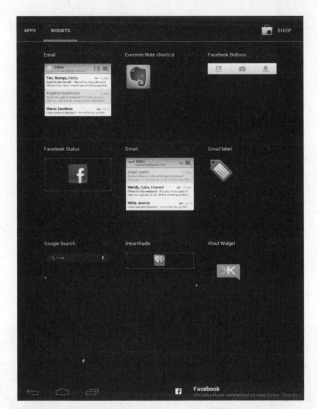

Figure 11-7: Klout Widget, shown on the Widgets menu.

2. **Tap and hold the widget to move it to your home screen.**

   A login screen appears.

3. **Enter your Twitter name (without the @ symbol) to log in as shown in Figure 11-8.**

Figure 11-8: Sign in via Twitter to operate Klout Widget.

Your Klout Widget now appears on your home screen displaying your updated Klout Score (see Figure 11-9).

Figure 11-9: Your Klout Score on your home screen.

Chapter 12

Operating Klout Using Apple Devices

In This Chapter

▶ Installing the Klout app on Apple Devices

▶ Logging in to your Klout account

▶ Viewing your Klout Score without opening the app

▶ Using Klout via your mobile profile

As Klout becomes more popular, it's also becoming more accessible. Klout has developed an app that you can download to Apple devices — such as iPhone, iPad, and iPod touch — to monitor some of the key features of the service.

Using Klout on your mobile devices can be useful when you want to check your Score, give another influencer +K on a topic, or monitor your profile. In some cases, showing the app at certain establishments can even get you a discount!

Downloading the Klout App

Before you download the Klout app for your Apple device, you need to sign up for a Klout account via Klout.com. Then you can download and sign in to the app.

Searching for the Klout app

Search for the Klout app by opening the App Store on your mobile device. Make sure the app you choose has been developed by Klout, and you can get started!

1. **Using your Apple device, open the App Store and tap Search from the options at the bottom of the screen.**

2. Enter Klout **in the search box.**

3. **Select Klout for iPhone (or iPad or iPod touch) by tapping the screenshot of the Klout logo (shown in Figure 12-1).**

Figure 12-1: View the Klout app via your mobile device.

Here, you can view the app details (shown in Figure 12-2) and read consumer reviews from other users to decide whether you wish to install this app. If you decide to add Klout to your mobile device, the process is simple.

Figure 12-2: Consumer reviews and app details are available in the App Store.

Installing Klout on iPad, iPhone, and iPod touch

Downloading Klout to your Apple device is as simple as tapping the Install button, shown in Figure 12-3.

Figure 12-3: Install the Klout app.

The installation process may take a couple of minutes. Afterward, the app appears on your home screen. Then simply tap the app icon to open the app and get started.

Connecting to Klout on Your iPhone or iPad

When you open Klout for the first time on your mobile device, you are prompted to sign in using either your existing Twitter or

Facebook account (as shown in Figure 12-4). You need to be logged in to whichever account you choose before you connect to Klout. If you aren't already logged in, a sign-in screen will appear for your network of choice.

Figure 12-4: Connect to Klout via Twitter or Facebook.

After you log in, you can read a little bit about the basics of Klout by swiping your finger from right to left across the screen. Klout provides little tips for improving your Score (as shown in Figure 12-5), a few influencers to follow, and a quick reference for giving +K to other influencers.

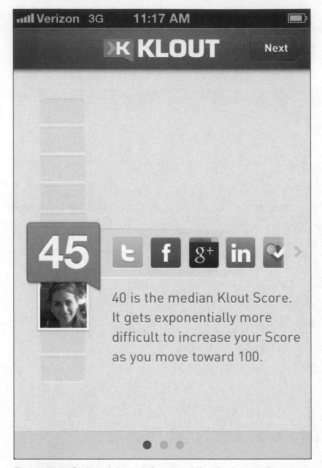

Figure 12-5: Swipe right to left to read tips for increasing your Klout Score.

After you log in to Klout on your mobile device, you are not able to return to the tips. This seems to be an oversight in the Klout app. Make sure to see what you want to see before you tap Get Started.

Tap the Get Started button to complete the login process.

Making the Most of Notifications

The Klout mobile experience is more limited than the full website. However, many features are still available with the mobile app, including giving +K to fellow influencers, checking your Klout Score, and making simple edits to your profile. And with the implementation of Klout for your iPhone Passbook you can even use Klout to get discounts and on-the-spot Perks in participating retail or entertainment locations. Passbook is an iPhone feature that uses participating apps from companies such as United Airlines and Target to allow you to keep tickets, reward cards, and coupons in one place.

The easiest way to make the most of your Klout app is to spend a few minutes getting familiar with all of its features, including the Notifications screen. Think of your Notifications screen as your inbox. Anything that happens regarding your Klout account appears on this page. Notifications refresh each time you open the Klout app, but you can manually refresh the screen at any time.

To refresh your notifications, drag your finger from the top of your screen to the bottom and release.

When you first open Klout with your iPhone or other Apple device (iPad, iPod touch), the first screen that appears is your Notifications screen. Here you see any recent activity that pertains to your Klout account (as shown in Figure 12-6). A menu item marked Notifications also appears at the bottom of your screen so you can return to this list at any time.

Potential notifications include

- ✔ **Changes in Klout Score:** When your Score rises or falls, you see a notification letting you know your most current Score.

- ✔ **New Perks for which you are eligible:** If you're eligible for a new Perk, you see a message on your Notifications screen.

- ✔ **New options for your mobile app:** When Klout makes changes or adds new features to the app, an alert appears.

- ✔ **Endorsements from other influencers:** Influencers that endorse you appear under notifications along with the topic for which they endorsed you.

The Notifications screen is interactive. Although it may simply look like a list of notifications, you can actually do quite a bit from this screen, including sending Tweets or Facebook messages, claiming Klout Perks, and viewing the profiles of other influencers. To act on a notification, first select the preferred alert and tap the arrow to the right of the message (as shown in Figure 12-6).

Tap an arrow for more options

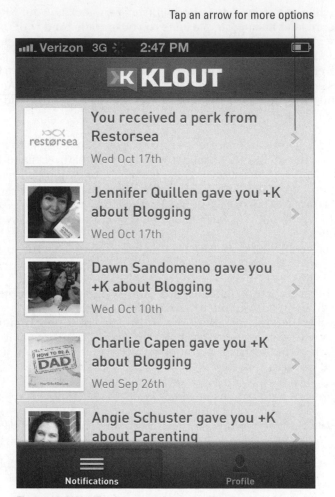

Figure 12-6: Notifications screen on the Klout app.

Creating a status update based on a notification

If you wish to respond to a notification with a Tweet or Facebook update, you can do so right from the Notifications screen.

1. **Select the desired notification by tapping the arrow to the right of the message.**

   A new screen appears with social media sharing buttons.

2. **Select the platform you wish to use (Twitter or Facebook) by tapping the appropriate button.**

   A pre-populated status message appears. You can submit this message as-is or make any desired edits.

3. **When you're ready, update your Twitter or Facebook status by tapping the Send button.**

You must also be signed in to Twitter or Facebook with your mobile device before you can make status updates from your Klout app.

Viewing an influencer's profile from the Notifications screen

If you receive an endorsement (+K) from another influencer, you are notified with his name and the topic(s) for which he endorsed you. From the Notifications screen, you can send a Tweet or Facebook status update to thank him for his endorsement using the instructions above. You can also view his profile.

Follow these steps to view another influencer's profile:

1. **Select the notification with the influencer you wish to view by tapping the arrow to the right of that message.**

   A screen appears with the topic for which you received +K and the social sharing buttons for Twitter and Facebook. A View Their Profile button is located at the bottom of the screen (Figure 12-7).

2. **Tap the View Their Profile button, which opens the influencer's profile in a new screen.**

When viewing another influencer's profile, you can tap her social media buttons to leave the Klout app and open a new social network, view who she influences and who she is influenced by, and give +K on one or more of her listed topics (as shown in Figure 12-8).

Figure 12-7: View an influencer's profile from the Notifications screen.

To endorse another influencer, swipe the orange arrow from left to right on one or more topics for which you wish to give +K.

Figure 12-8: Swipe from left to right to give +K to another influencer.

Claiming a Perk from the Notifications screen

If you see a notification that you have received a Klout Perk, you don't have to wait until you log in to your computer. You can claim the Perk right from your phone!

Claim a Perk from your mobile device by following these steps:

1. **Select the Perk you wish to claim by tapping the arrow to the right of the Perk information.**

A new screen appears with more information about the Perk as shown in Figure 12-9.

Figure 12-9: Claim your Perk.

2. **Tap the Claim Your Perk button.**

3. **Follow the instructions to verify your address information and tap Submit.**

If the Perk is full or has expired, you can't claim it. Instead, you see a message that looks similar to the one in Figure 12-10. If you don't want to miss any Perks, make sure to check in with Klout on a regular basis.

Figure 12-10: This Perk is no longer available.

Adding Klout to your iPhone Passbook

Occasionally, Klout partners with restaurants and/or hotels to provide in-person Perks or discounts. If you become eligible for one of these special treats, you're asked to show your Klout *card*, which is simply your name and Klout Score along with a QR code for the establishment to scan. A *QR (quick response) code* is somewhat similar to a bar code.

To add Klout to your Passbook

1. Open your Klout Notifications screen.

2. **Tap the Add Klout to Passbook notification.**

   A new screen appears (as shown in Figure 12-11).

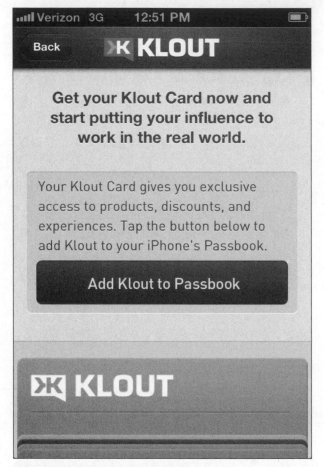

Figure 12-11: Add Klout to your Passbook.

3. **Tap the Add Klout to Passbook button.**

   Your card appears (shown in Figure 12-12).

4. **Tap the Add button in the top-right corner to add or update your card.**

Figure 12-12: A Klout Passbook card.

A confirmation screen appears (as shown in Figure 12-13) when you have successfully added your Klout card to your Passbook.

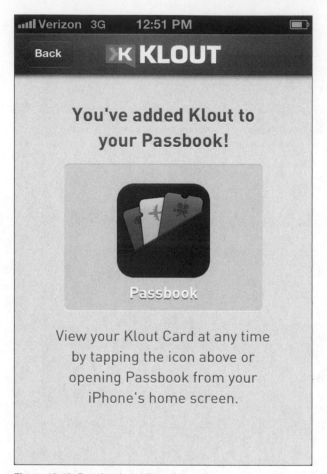

Figure 12-13: Passbook confirmation.

Understanding Your Mobile Klout Profile

Next to the Notifications button at the bottom of your screen, you see a Profile icon. Tapping this button takes you to your personal Klout Profile screen (as shown in Figure 12-14).

Figure 12-14: A Klout profile.

From this screen, you can view your topics, influencers, and people you influence and make simple edits to your profile information. You can also connect with certain social networks from the mobile app. However, at this time the option to disconnect from these networks is available only by using the full online version.

The Klout Profile screen also includes access to the Settings screen, from which you can set up Push Notifications (notifications that pop up in real time on your home screen even when the app isn't open), pin your Score to your home screen, log out, and send feedback to the Klout staff.

Updating your profile with the Klout app

You can make minor edits from your mobile profile such as updating your bio, removing topics, and adding social networks. However, at this time you are not able to change your profile picture or add topics via the mobile app.

If you wish to change your bio, the process is simple:

1. **Open the Klout app, and then open your profile by tapping the Profile button at the bottom-right of your screen.**

2. **Tap the Edit button in the upper-right corner of your profile.**

   The area around your bio turns from gray to white as shown in Figure 12-15.

3. **Tap the white screen where your bio is located and make changes as desired.**

4. **To save your new bio, tap the Done button in the upper-right corner of the screen.**

You may also wish to remove certain topics or influencers from your profile. You can do that from the mobile app as well.

To remove items from your Klout profile

1. **Open the Klout app and open your profile by tapping the Profile button at the bottom-right of your screen.**

2. **Tap the Edit button in the upper-right corner of your profile.**

   Small black circles containing white *x*s appear above your Klout connections and topics.

3. **To remove a contact or topic, tap the corresponding *x* above that item.**

   A confirmation warning appears (as shown in Figure 12-16).

4. **If you're sure you want to delete this person or topic from your profile, tap the red Delete button.**

   Or you can tap Cancel if you wish to end this process without making any changes.

5. **When you're done making edits, tap the Done button in the upper-right corner of your screen.**

Figure 12-15: Edit your Klout bio.

Figure 12-16: Choose Delete or Cancel in the confirmation warning.

Adding a social network

Klout offers the ability to connect with your other social networks (including Facebook, Twitter, and foursquare) via its mobile app. The social networks you can connect are limited in the mobile app, but a handful is available to get you started.

To find out if the app has an available social network that you haven't yet connected, view the network icons at the top of your Profile screen. A network that's already connected has an icon in full color. A network that hasn't yet been connected is faded and also has a plus (+) sign in the upper-right corner.

To add a social network to your Klout mobile profile

1. **Open the Klout app and open your profile by tapping the Profile button at the bottom-right of your screen.**

2. **Use your finger to slide the social network icons until you find the one you wish to add.**

3. **Select the social network you wish to add by tapping the icon with the plus sign (shown in Figure 12-17).**

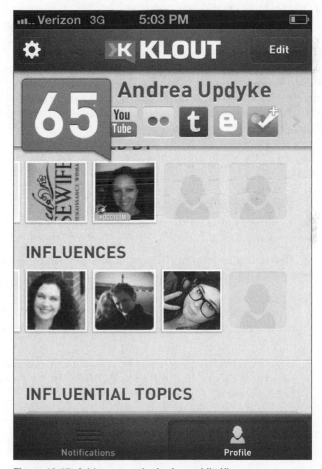

Figure 12-17: Add a network via the mobile Klout app.

4. **Log in to the social network (if necessary).**

   After you log in, grant access or allow Klout to connect with your social network.

   You are now connected, and the social network icon is in full color on your mobile app.

You may remove any of your connected networks by logging in to the full website at Klout.com.

Displaying your Klout Score on your home screen

Your Klout Score is updated on a daily basis. You can choose to be alerted of these changes in real time in two ways. You can turn on Push Notifications that alert you to Score changes with a pop-up message on your phone. Or you can choose to display your Klout Score on your home screen. If you choose the latter, your Score will always be displayed in a small red box above your Klout app icon.

To turn on Push Notifications and/or display your Score in your home screen

1. **Open the Klout App.**

2. **Tap the Profile icon in the bottom-right corner of your screen.**

3. **Tap the gear icon in the upper-left corner to open your app's settings page (shown in Figure 12-18).**

4. **Tap the On/Off button next to the Tell Me About Score Changes option and/or the Tell Me When I Get +K option to receive pop-up notifications on your home screen in real time.**

5. **If you wish to display your Score on the home screen (as shown in Figure 12-19), tap the On/Off button next to the Set App Badge to Klout Score option.**

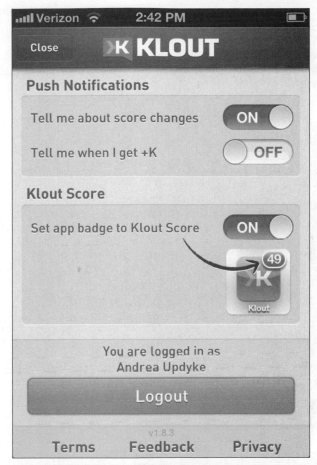

Figure 12-18: Change Push Notification settings.

Exploring other features on the Settings screen

The Klout Settings screen also contains a few important documents at a glance. You can view Klout's terms of service and privacy policy or send an e-mail with feedback by tapping one of the buttons at the bottom of the Settings screen.

If you wish to log out of your Klout app, you can do it from the Settings screen. To do so, simply tap the Logout button.

Figure 12-19: Your Klout Score appears on your home screen.

Chapter 13

Leveraging Klout as a Brand

•••

In This Chapter

▶ Connecting your brand with influencers

▶ Deciphering the Perks process

▶ Navigating the pros and cons of running a Perk

▶ Discovering Klout for Business

•••

*I*f you represent a brand, whether it's a large corporation or a small business, you can use Klout to get your message out and create buzz about your product. Klout believes that drilling down by topics of interest as well as Klout Scores allows brands to benefit from positive reviews and word-of-mouth product endorsements.

Brands can create Perks, run Klout for Good campaigns (which I tell you about in Chapter 9), and interact with influencers in an organic way by using Klout. There is still some discussion about how effective Perks programs are to sales in the long run, but the bottom line is it's always a good thing when people are sharing information and talking about your brand online or offline. According to Klout, each person who receives a Perk can generate up to 30 pieces of content and 100,000 impressions for your product. And brands are definitely taking notice.

In this chapter, you learn how to use Klout to build brand influence, understand the basics of running a Klout Perk, and implement lists to organize influencers by Klout Score or topic of influence. You can also learn to communicate with your followers and show them your brand appreciation by endorsing them with +K. Finally, I tell you about the Klout for Business website.

Building Your Brand's Influence

If your brand is just getting started with Klout, the first step is to connect your social networks to Klout, which I tell you how to do in Chapter 2. Having a strong social media presence is important when building brand buzz. Klout users are typically very Internet savvy and expect brands to be as well.

Make sure your brand bio is complete and interesting to engage influencers and keep them coming back for more. Then you will be ready to build your Klout presence by searching for and endorsing other influencers. There are several ways you can do this via Klout, which I discuss in this section.

Finding influencers

After your brand's social media accounts are connected to Klout, you can begin to search for influencers you wish to connect with. You can search by name, Klout Score, or topic of influence, depending on your need.

Interactions on the Klout website itself are limited, so you still need to rely on your other social media networks (such as Twitter, Facebook, and Google+) to interact with your followers. Still, you can endorse others and create lists for influencers using Klout, and this may prove beneficial if you decide to run a Klout Perk for your brand.

Viewing Influencers from Facebook and Twitter

When you connect your social networks to Klout, you are automatically connected with influencers you follow and connect with on your social networks (like Twitter and Facebook). You can view these users by clicking Friends on the navigation bar at the top of your Klout page (shown in Figure 13-1).

After you've clicked Friends, you can view your fellow influencers a number of ways. First, this is a list of influencers *you* follow, not those who follow you or your brand.

As indicated in the sidebar on the left side of your screen (shown in Figure 13-2), influencers you follow are sorted based on the network on which you follow them. Currently, you can view influencers via your connected Twitter and Facebook accounts.

Friends

Figure 13-1: Click Friends on the navigation bar.

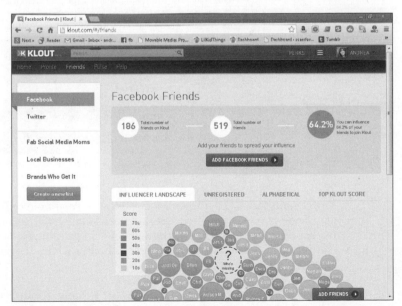

Figure 13-2: Sort influencers from either Twitter or Facebook connections.

To view influencers connected from Facebook, follow these steps:

1. **Log in to Klout.com by signing in to the site in the upper-right corner of the screen.**

2. **Point your browser to your Friends page by clicking Friends on the navigation bar at the top of the page.**

3. **Select Facebook from the sidebar on the left side of the screen.**

   The main screen populates with user information and options for sorting influencers (Influencer Landscape, Unregistered, Alphabetical, and Top Klout Score) as shown in Figure 13-3.

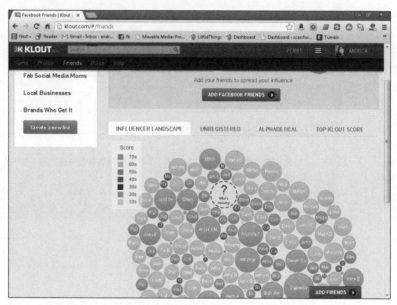

Figure 13-3: Facebook influencer information.

The default tab is the Influencer Landscape. Available only for Facebook connections, this interactive screen sorts your influencers by Score using eye-catching, colorful graphics (shown in Figure 13-4). The larger dots represent higher Klout Scores and the smaller dots represent lower Scores.

Hover over any dot to view an influencer's name, Klout Score, and connected networks (shown in Figure 13-5). You may also click a dot to open that influencer's Profile page.

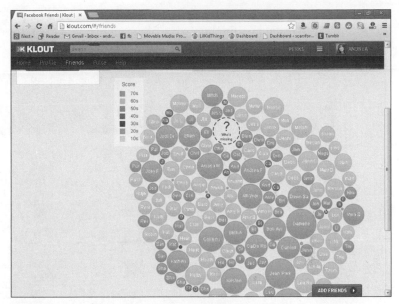

Figure 13-4: Facebook Influencer Landscape.

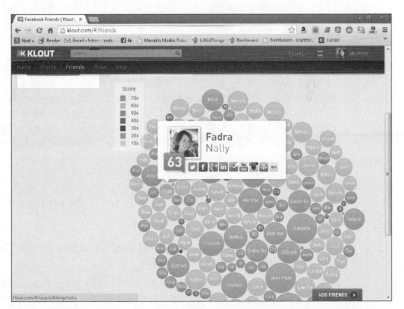

Figure 13-5: View more influencer information by hovering the mouse pointer over any dot in the graph.

To view influencers by Top Klout Score, select the Top Score tab on the Facebook Friends page. Your influencers are sorted by Klout Score from highest to lowest (as shown in Figure 13-6).

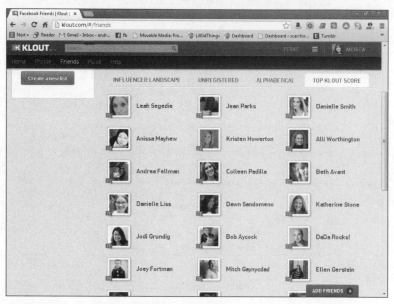

Figure 13-6: Top influencers sorted by Klout Score.

As a brand looking to interact with social media influencers, looking at influencers with the highest Klout Score may be helpful in determining who might make a good match for your brand. Remember that Klout Scores are only one measure of influence, but as a part of a bigger picture, can shed light on many users who might not otherwise be in the spotlight but are really great at engaging their communities.

To view influencers connected via Twitter, the process is similar to finding Facebook friends.

1. **Log in to Klout.com by signing in to the site in the upper-right corner of the screen.**

2. **Point your browser to your Friends page by clicking Friends on the navigation bar at the top of the page.**

3. **Select Twitter from the sidebar on the left side of the screen.**

   Your Twitter influencers have only two sorting options (Recently Followed and Highest Klout Score) on the main screen as shown in Figure 13-7.

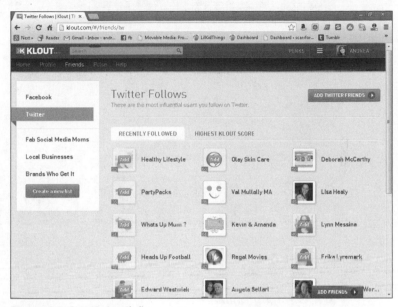

Figure 13-7: Sort Twitter influencers.

You can sort by Twitter users you've recently followed as well as by Klout Score using the tabs at the top of the screen. Click any of the icons to view the Profile page for a particular user.

Using Klout Pulse to search for top influencers

Klout uses a feature called Klout Pulse to harvest the Internet's top influencers in specific fields like athletics, politics, and entertainment. Klout highlights current events and hot topics in its Klout Pulse categories, and this is a great way to find out how some of the most influential people on the web use social media.When you click a Pulse category, you see a ranking of the top influencers in that category, each influencer's Klout Score, links to each influencer's Klout profile and social media accounts, and a recent post.

Click Pulse from the navigation bar at the top of the screen to view these top performer lists curated by Klout (shown in Figure 13-8).

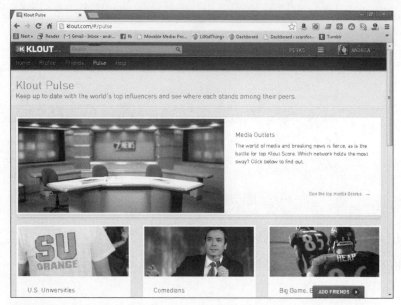

Figure 13-8: Use Klout Pulse to view top influencers from across the web.

Searching by topic

If you're looking to connect with influencers based on a specific topic of influence, you can do so by using Klout's Search feature. Take this a step further and curate a Klout list of these influencers for future campaigns.

To find influencers by topic

1. **Log in to Klout.com using the sign-on in the upper-right corner of the screen.**

2. **Using the search field at the top of your screen, type in a one-word topic and press the Enter key (or click the magnifying glass).**

   A new page populates containing the top influencers in that topic as well as the top Moments related to that topic, as shown in Figure 13-9.

3. **Select any influencer and view her profile by clicking the icon containing her avatar.**

If you wish to group certain influencers together for future reference, consider making a list on the Friends page.

Figure 13-9: Top influencers and Moments related to the topic of blogging.

To make a list, you need to know a user's Twitter name. To stream-line this process, you might want to have two browser windows open at the same time, one with your search results and one with the list you're creating. Hopefully in the future, Klout will add an "add to list" feature to every influencer's profile. But that's cur-rently not the case.

Create a list by following these steps:

1. **Gather the Twitter names of the influencers you wish to add to your new list.**

2. **Log in to Klout using the sign-in button in the upper-right corner of the screen.**

3. **Open the Friends page by clicking Friends on the naviga-tion menu.**

4. **Open the list function by selecting the orange Create a New List button.**

   A pop-up window appears (shown in Figure 13-10).

5. **Add influencers to your list by typing their Twitter names in the Add People field and clicking Add.**

   Don't include the @ symbol with the influencer's Twitter handle.

6. **Name your list and add a description if desired, as shown in Figure 13-11, and save your list by clicking Save.**

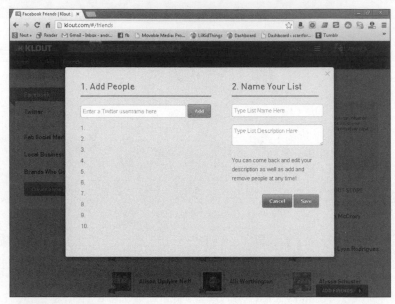

Figure 13-10: Create a new list.

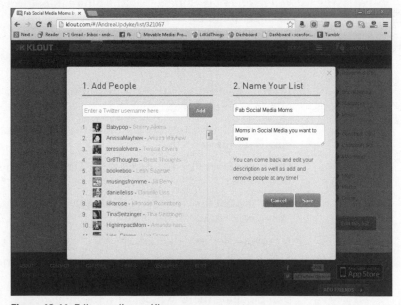

Figure 13-11: Edit your list on Klout.

You have now created a new list that appears in the sidebar on the left of your screen. You can edit this list at any time by opening the list and clicking Edit.

Another feature you'll notice after you create your list is the addition of Klout topics and the opportunity to endorse influencers in these topics. This is a great way to show appreciation to an influencer and help him increase his Score.

Paying it forward through Klout

Part of the magic of using social media effectively as a brand is finding the sweet spot between marketing and promotion and authentic conversation. As you build your network and find influencers that are a good fit for your brand, pay it forward by endorsing their expertise in a particular topic. In Klout, this is called giving +K, and I discuss the concept in detail in Chapter 7. Recognizing influencers for their hard work goes a long way, and it couldn't be easier.

To give +K to another influencer, you can do so in one of two ways:

1. **Log in to Klout in the upper-right corner of your screen.**

2. **Search for an influencer by name and click Give +K next to one of the topics you wish to endorse in the left-hand sidebar.**

Or

1. **Log in to Klout in the upper-right corner of your screen.**

2. **Open a list by clicking Friends on the navigation bar at the top of your screen and choosing a list from the left-hand sidebar.**

3. **Scroll to the influencer you wish to endorse and click Give +K next to the topic you wish to endorse.**

As you continue to build relationships with other influencers and brands, you'll see authentic working relationships emerge and grow.

Running a Perk

If Klout is known for one thing, it's definitely the Perks. Influencers love to sign in and find a new Perk notification in their profiles. Brands love the organic word-of-mouth endorsements that happen when people enjoy their Perks. In short, everybody wins to a degree. Not all Perks are equal, and as a brand, it's important to make sure you don't overspend. Marketing based on perceived influence is somewhat controversial. The jury is still out on whether or not so-called influence and buzz translate into sales. However, many brands have benefitted from promoting their new products and/or services using Klout Perks.

Rather than simply throwing free goodies to the masses, Klout offers brands a way to target users based on their topics of influence, demographics, age, gender, and Klout Score. In turn, brand promotions are targeted to the people who'll actually talk about them and take the time to provide quality feedback to the brand. Of course, if your brand's goal is to reach a high number of people, you want fewer restrictions when you create your Perk.

No two campaigns are alike and for this reason, Klout is happy to answer questions and help brands customize the Perks program that's right for them.

Brands interested in working with Klout to create a Perk should send an e-mail to `partners@klout.com` for more information and a consultation.

If you're interested in learning more about running a Klout Perk, I share a few case studies to give you a bird's eye view on how the system works. Because each Perk is different, Klout offers different approaches to make the most of your experience.

Reviewing past Klout Perks

Take a look at some brands that have partnered with Klout in the past with targeted Perks campaigns. By adding the element of social sharing to the mix, brands were able to distribute their products and create valuable, organic word-of-mouth marketing campaigns in the process. Big names like Disney, Nike, and American Express have participated in Perks programs with good results.

When Disney ran a promotion for the movie *Tangled,* it invited influential moms and dads to attend an early screening of the movie with their children and provided them with some other free goodies. In turn, the 455 influencers generated more than

39 million impressions for the campaign and more than 15,000 Tweets (as shown in Figure 13-12).

Figure 13-12: Disney's *Tangled* campaign with Klout.

But when you're talking about Disney, whose movies are widely anticipated and celebrated before they're even released, it seemed like a good bet that a Klout campaign featuring an early screening of *Tangled* would do well.

But chances are most brands don't have the big budgets or the name recognition that major corporations can leverage. So where does that leave the smaller or lesser-known businesses?

Learning Klout Perks through trial-and-error

Morgan Brown, the Director of Social Media for an online discount-ticket purchasing site called ScoreBig.com (Figure 13-13), has written about two separate campaigns he participated in through Klout. And although Klout's pricing structure and Perks programming is specific to each case, the information Brown provides can be helpful when deciding how to approach a new Perks campaign.

In the first campaign, the brand spent a good amount of time and money targeting influencers with high Scores and a specific geographic location. The folks at ScoreBig gave a quality Perk with a referral bonus to targeted users to encourage a high number of shares.

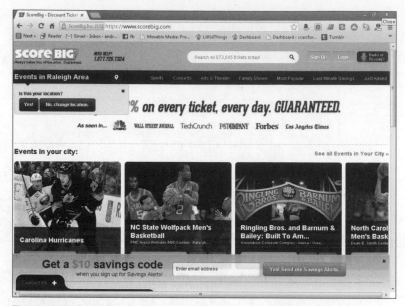

Figure 13-13: ScoreBig.com.

However, the ultimate return on their investment was not nearly what they had hoped for. Because their goal was to acquire new customers, they discovered that a broader approach would better meet the needs of the brand. As Brown shares, Klout worked with them a second time to formulate a new campaign that looked quite different.

In the second scenario, Klout Score was not the main criteria for inclusion in the Perk. Instead, a lesser amount was gifted to a much larger number of influencers, which resulted in 40 times the social shares of the original campaign and 3 times the number of impressions (shown in Figure 13-14).

Brown's conclusion was that in the case of his brand that was looking to gain new customers, Klout Scores weren't as important as actual users testing out the product. He also found that Klout users were ready and willing to spread the word about a Perk they loved. However, if a brand's goal is brand building, a higher influencer Score may be useful to target a specific audience.

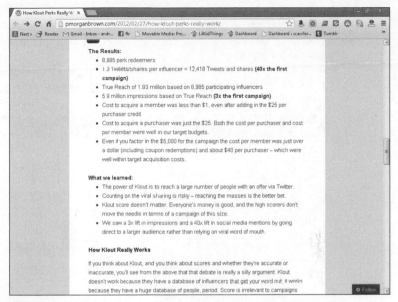

Figure 13-14: Results comparison from two separate brand campaigns.

To read Brown's entire analysis, visit his post, "How Klout Perks Really Work" at

```
http://pmorganbrown.com/2012/02/27/how-klout-perks-
really-work.
```

Identifying a product that speaks to everyone

The now widely known music-sharing service, Spotify (Figure 13-15), had excellent results from its Klout Perks campaign. In fact, I was one of the beneficiaries of this particular Klout Perk, and not only did I hear about Spotify for the first time through Klout, I also saw several tweets and conversations surrounding this Perks program, which is exactly the point.

It should come as no surprise though because the campaign engaged more than 92,000 influencers and garnered 291 million impressions (shown in Figure 13-16) by the end of the Perk. Spotify is here to stay. And with its merge with Facebook, its growth seems boundless.

The fact is, everyone likes music. And with a product like Spotify that offered a free service to all and a premium service in the way of Perks to selected influencers, the odds of success were definitely in its favor.

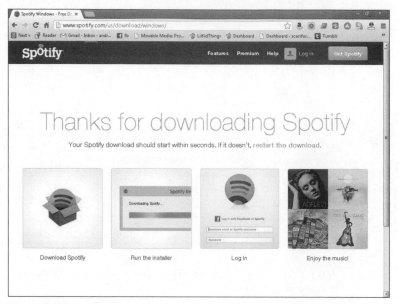

Figure 13-15: Spotify.com.

Figure 13-16: Case study of Spotify's Klout campaign.

Obtaining feedback on a Perk

Another benefit to running a Perk through Klout is its feedback model. After an influencer accepts a Perk, Klout prompts him for feedback after he's had a chance to try the product or service.

Giving feedback is easy and often enjoyable for an influencer who loved her Perk. Likewise, if she had an issue or was dissatisfied with the product, she won't have any issues sharing that information in the feedback section.

Brands benefit from this honest feedback without having to do the dirty work of collecting the information.

Giving feedback on a Perk looks like this: After an influencer claims a Perk, a notification appears letting her know that the brand would love feedback. A pop-up window appears with questions specific to the Perk. Influencers have the chance to rate the Perk from one to five stars, leave a review, and even upload a photo of them using the Perk (shown in Figure 13-17). Influencers are also prompted to connect with the brand via social networks like Facebook or Twitter.

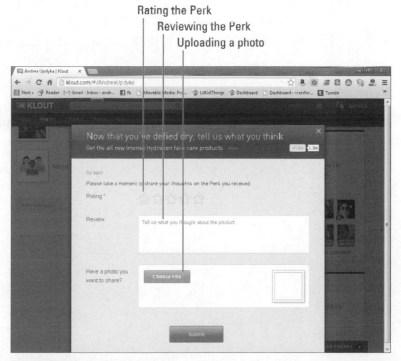

Figure 13-17: Perks Feedback page.

If you decide to run a Klout Perk, Klout will provide you with a full report including metrics and feedback when the promotion is finished.

Finding more info on Perks

You need to consider a number of factors when choosing whether a Perks program is right for your brand. For more in-depth analysis of how Klout has performed in the industry, take a look at these helpful articles:

- ✔ "The World's 50 Most Innovative Companies," at

    www.fastcompany.com/most-innovative-companies/
    2012/industry/advertising#klout

- ✔ "Got Klout?: Why a Klout Perks Campaign Might Work for Your Brand," at

    www.talentzoo.com/beneath-the-brand/blog_news.
    php?articleID=11403

- ✔ "Do Klout Perks carry any real-world weight?," at

    www.pcworld.com/article/262193/do-klout-perks-
    carry-any-real-world-weight.html

- ✔ "Your Social Influence and Why Marketers Care about It," at

    http://mashable.com/2012/06/08/social-influence-
    klout

For an intro to Klout, check out this instructional video that walks you through the process, including analytics and campaign statistics available to the brand (shown in Figure 13-18) at

    www.youtube.com/watch?v=GY1EJuFIY_U&feature=
    youtu.be

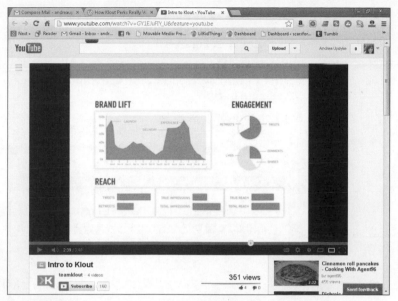

Figure 13-18: Example of a Perks campaign report from Klout.

Introducing Klout for Business

At the time this book first went to the printer, Klout announced a new platform solely for businesses, called Klout for Business. Still in beta, Klout for Business will give even more insights for businesses and brands looking to benefit from the massive data Klout is collecting.

Getting started with Klout for Business

To connect your business to Klout for Business, your business needs to be active on Twitter and have a Facebook Page for the business (not a Facebook profile, which is for personal use).

Klout for Business is rolling out a little bit at a time and asking that those who are interested in the service request access to use the serviceas follows:

1. **Point your browser to** http://klout.com/s/business.

2. **Click the blue button Let's Get Started button.**

3. **Enter your name and business information, as well as your e-mail address into the pop-up window that appears (as shown in Figure 13-19).**

4. **Select the check box that says, "I'd like to be one of the first to gain access to Klout's revolutionary new business insights portal."**

5. **Click Submit.**

Figure 13-19: Request access to Klout for Business.

Learning about Klout for Business

As Klout refines this new service and you're waiting for access, you can check in with Klout for Business by visiting ther website at `http://klout.com/s/business` to check out what they have in store for brands.

On this site, you can dig deeper into the Klout machine and learn about the following:

- ✔ Case studies from past Perks programs
- ✔ Press mentions
- ✔ Return on influence

Klout for Business is growing and changing every day, so make sure to check back for more information and sign up your brand for this new service.

Chapter 14

Ten Influencers to Watch

● ●

In This Chapter

▶ Ten Influencers to connect with in social media

▶ Why you should follow these influencers

● ●

The social media space is vibrant and alive with influencers from all over the world who are using their voices to make a difference. These influencers invest time and thought to help their followers laugh, think, and build their businesses.

By glancing at Klout Scores, you can get a quick idea of who may or may not be particularly influential. But remember that Scores are based on public information and the influencer's participation. For this reason, it's also important to take a look around an influencer's various social networks to get an idea of how she interacts with her communities.

I created a list of ten notable influencers who engage with their followers in meaningful ways, are a consistent presence across social media networks (like Facebook and Twitter), and provide a valuable service to their followers. These influencers have great Klout Scores, but more importantly, they set excellent examples for how to use social media effectively. Of course, countless influencers are doing it right, so this list is by no means complete. Use these ten people as a starting point and go from there.

Guy Kawasaki

Guy Kawasaki (shown in Figure 14-1) is a best-selling author, blogger, and co-founder of www.alltop.com. With hundreds of thousands of followers across his social media networks, Guy is an influencer you don't want to miss.

Kawasaki has a Klout Score of 87. You can find him on Facebook, Twitter, and Google+ (as shown in Figure 14-2) where he created a community called APE for authors, publishers, and entrepreneurs where he engages with and encourages his followers.

Figure 14-1: Klout profile for Guy Kawasaki.

Figure 14-2: Guy Kawasaki on Google+.

Danielle Smith

Danielle (shown in Figure 14-3) is an author, blogger, and video correspondent. She not only has an impressive list of credentials, but she takes the time to interact with her community with sincerity on a regular basis.

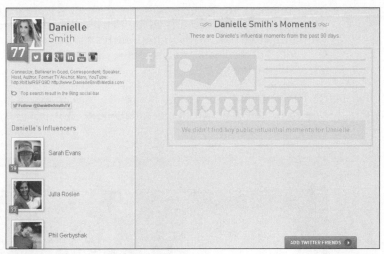

Figure 14-3: Klout profile for Danielle Smith.

Danielle is an encourager and contributes her thoughts in a nonconfrontational way while being willing to discuss important issues in our culture. She has a Klout Score of 77 and can be found online at http://daniellesmithmedia.com (as shown in Figure 14-4).

Figure 14-4: Danielle Smith Media.

Gary Vaynerchuk

Gary, known as @garyvee on Twitter (shown in Figure 14-5), regularly engages his community of almost 1 million followers in a fun yet informative way. With an impressive résumé and extensive knowledge of the social media scene, Gary comes across as a regular, family-loving guy.

Gary Vaynerchuk has a Klout Score of 82 (as shown in Figure 14-6). You can connect with him using the above Twitter name or on his Facebook Page at www.facebook.com/gary.

Figure 14-5: @garyvee on Twitter.

Figure 14-6: Gary Vaynerchuk on Klout.

Young House Love

John and Sherry Petersik are a husband-and-wife team from Virginia who just wanted to fix up their first home and document their progress. What they ended up with was a successful blog that spawned an incredible online following and a book deal. Their joint account has a Klout Score of 73 (as shown in Figure 14-7).

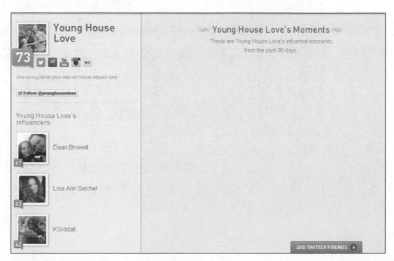

Figure 14-7: Young House Love on Klout.

The Petersiks are great to watch because they do an excellent job of relating to the DIY community and talking about family life while at the same time contributing to the social media scene. They are now renovating their second home, and you can follow their journey at www.younghouselove.com.

Darren Rowse

As the founder of Problogger.com (shown in Figure 14-8), Darren Rowse seems to be the definition of good social media strategy for many bloggers. His knowledge of best practices and social media tips is a seemingly never-ending well.

Rowse is an all-around helpful person, which is another reason he is one to watch. With a Klout Score of 83 (shown in Figure 14-9), you can be sure Darren is engaging his community with consistency. Learn more about Darren on ProBlogger at www.problogger.net/about-darren.

Figure 14-8: ProBlogger founded by Darren Rowse.

Figure 14-9: Klout Score for Darren Rowse.

Jeremy Cowart

Photographer, artist, and founder of Help-Portrait, Jeremy Cowart (shown in Figure 14-10) is definitely an influencer of many. Through his organization, he engages his community in a way that has inspired thousands of photographers to give their time and resources to provide family portraits for those who are not able to afford them.

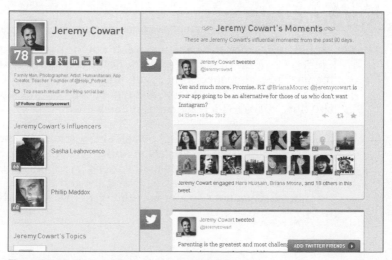

Figure 14-10: Klout profile page for Jeremy Cowart.

Jeremy has a Klout Score of 78, and his account for Help-Portrait has a Score of 69. You can find Jeremy on Twitter at `https://twitter.com/jeremycowart` (shown in Figure 14-11), and check out the Help-Portrait website at `http://help-portrait.com`.

Figure 14-11: Jeremy Cowart on Twitter.

Kelby Carr

As a blogger, an author, and the creator of the Type-A Parent Conference (shown in Figure 14-12), Kelby is no stranger to social media. She built a successful community website for parents and ultimately the conference that has influenced countless bloggers and businesses to increase their online value.

Kelby engages her community by asking questions and having conversations across all her social networks. She connects with her followers and responds to them in a friendly manner. Kelby's Klout Score is 69 (shown in Figure 14-13) and she can be found tweeting from her @typeamom Twitter account or her website, located at `http://typeaparent.com`.

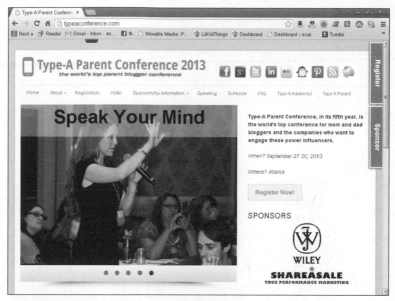

Figure 14-12: The Type-A Parent Conference website.

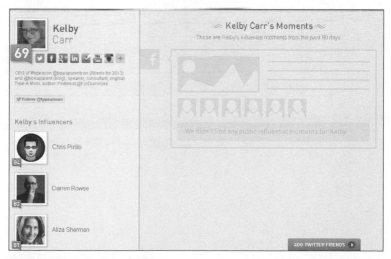

Figure 14-13: Kelby Carr on Klout.

Peter Shankman

Peter Shankman (shown in Figure 14-14) is an author and the founder of the wildly successful website, HARO (Help A Reporter Out, www.helpareporter.com). He spends his time consulting and speaking about marketing and social media. He approaches the online world with the attitude that "having an audience is a privilege, not a right" and he interacts with his community with that in mind.

Figure 14-14: Klout profile for Peter Shankman.

Peter Shankman has a Klout Score of 80 and can be found all over the Internet chatting with people and creating content. Get to know Peter at http://shankman.com (shown in Figure 14-15).

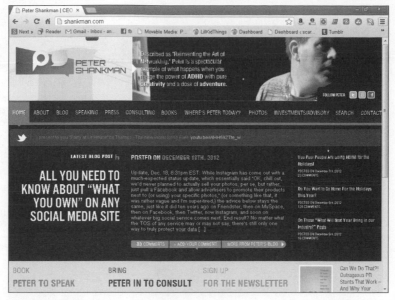

Figure 14-15: Shankman.com.

Ricky Gervais

I included Ricky Gervais because he has done a remarkable job of using social media to interact with his followers despite his celebrity status. Not only does he maintain his sense of humor, but he is also a businessman. Ricky is the co-founder of the Just Sayin' app (shown in Figure 14-16) that aims to bring the power of voice into the social web.

Ricky believes that some things are better heard than read, and if you've ever listened to one of his podcasts, I bet you'll agree! Gervais has a Klout Score of 89 (shown in Figure 14-17). Find him on Twitter at `https://twitter.com/rickygervais` and check out the Just Sayin' app on its website `www.justsayinapp.com`.

Figure 14-16: Just Sayin' App from Ricky Gervais.

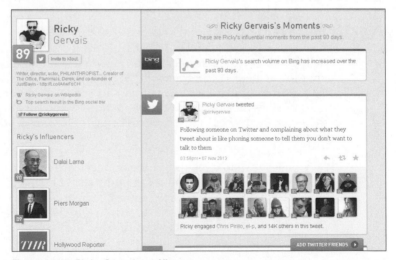

Figure 14-17: Ricky Gervais on Klout.

Amber Naslund

Amber Naslund (shown in Figure 14-18) is a social business con-
sultant, speaker, and co-author of the book The NOW Revolution.
Amber uses her voice to inspire businesses to embrace the human

connections within the social media space. She teaches that the tools we have online can be made even greater by keeping our interactions personal and accessible.

Figure 14-18: Amber Naslund on Klout.

Amber has a Klout Score of 67 and can be found online at www. brasstackthinking.com (shown in Figure 14-19).

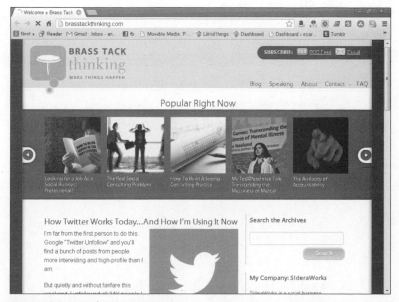

Figure 14-19: Brass Tack Thinking.

Chapter 15

Ten Brands To Watch

*1*nfluencers come in all shapes and sizes. Some are simply connecting recreationally, while others are brands with full-on social media strategies and departments dedicated to serving their customers through their social media channels. Brands connect with consumers on Twitter and Facebook, through blogs, and even on YouTube.

A brand that "gets it" is one that can promote its service or product while maintaining the personal banter and connection of a friendship. Some brands are better at this than others, just like people.

My collection of ten brands to watch includes brands that do a great job of listening to their consumers and keeping the lines of communication open. Whether their social media accounts are run by one person or a social media team, these ten brands have mastered the art of keeping the social in social media.

Ford Motor Company

The Ford social media accounts are run by Scott Monty and Karen Untereker, and they do a great job of providing great content and responding to consumers. They promote Ford consistently, but they also create conversations around trends in the automobile industry and share articles that are relevant to the brand. Ford Motor Company has a Klout Score of 92 (see Figure 15-1) and a strong presence on both Twitter and Facebook.

Fans are invited to share photos of their Fords in action on the company Facebook Page. You can connect with Ford on Twitter at `https://twitter.com/Ford` and Facebook at `www.facebook.com/ford` (see Figure 15-2).

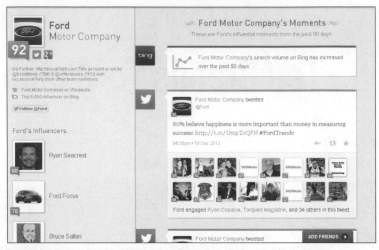

Figure 15-1: Ford Motor Company on Klout.

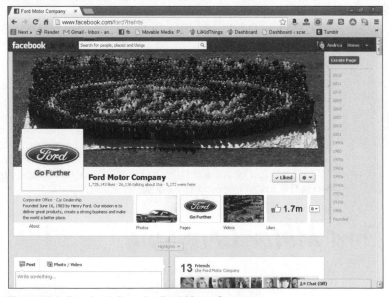

Figure 15-2: Facebook Page for Ford Motor Company.

Chobani

Chobani yogurt (shown on Klout in Figure 15-3) has had some recognition for its activity on Pinterest (a visual social networking and bookmarking site) and has built an active community around its yogurt brand. The folks at Chobani are sharing recipes and answering questions from their community with consistency and enthusiasm. Doing so connects them to their customers, and that can only be a good thing.

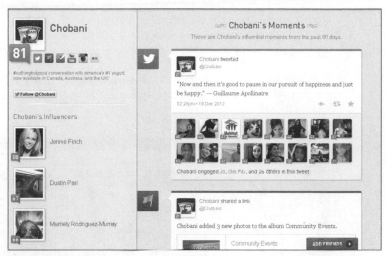

Figure 15-3: Klout profile for Chobani.

Chobani's Klout Score is 81. You can follow the company on Twitter at https://twitter.com/Chobani and check out its Pinterest boards at http://pinterest.com/chobani/ (see Figure 15-4).

Figure 15-4: Chobani on Pinterest.

Gap

Many fashion-related brands are doing a great job creating social media content for their brand. Gap uses Twitter, Facebook, Pinterest, and Instagram (shown in Figure 15-5) to share deals and high-quality images of its products while at the same time creating relevant conversations and connecting with its customers.

Gap has a Klout Score of 86 (as shown in Figure 15-6). Follow Gap on Instagram at `http://instagram.com/gap/` and Facebook at `www.facebook.com/gap`.

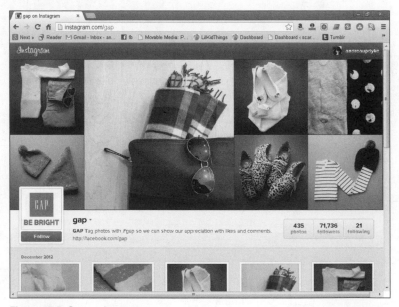

Figure 15-5: Gap on Instagram.

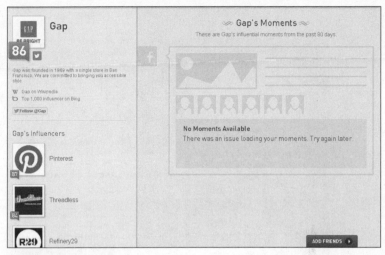

Figure 15-6: Gap on Klout.com.

Old Spice

If you enjoy the Old Spice commercials that have been on the air in the past couple of years ("I'm on a horse."), then you'll love its Twitter account (shown in Figure 15-7). Old Spice has raised the bar for other brands by using humor to keep people coming back for more. Who knew deodorant could be so funny?

The Klout Score for Old Spice is 82 (as shown in Figure 15-8), and the company can be found on Twitter at `https://twitter.com/OldSpice` and YouTube at `www.youtube.com/OldSpice`.

Figure 15-7: Twitter account for Old Spice.

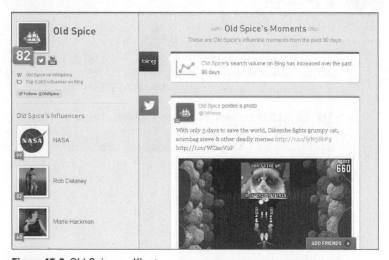

Figure 15-8: Old Spice on Klout.

McDonald's

Food chains are a natural fit for the world of social media because they have built-in fans. And McDonald's has a lot of fans. Its social media team manages the Twitter account for McDonald's (shown in Figure 15-9) with optimism and goodwill.

Figure 15-9: McDonald's Twitter account.

McDonald's has a Klout Score of 91 (shown in Figure 15-10), and you can find it on Twitter at `https://twitter.com/McDonalds`. You can also get to know the team behind the tweets by visiting the team page at `www.aboutmcdonalds.com/mcd/newsroom/ meet_the_tweeps_mcdonalds_twitter_team.html`.

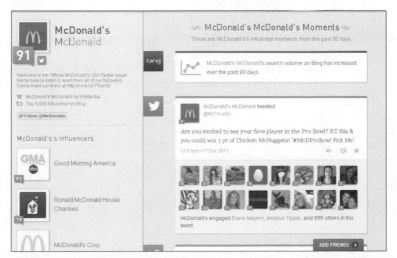

Figure 15-10: Klout page for McDonald's.

Best Buy

I have personally dealt with Best Buy via its Twitter account (shown in Figure 15-11) and it was a huge success. There were people ready to go when I had a question and they were very pleasant to deal with. Some individual stores also have their own accounts, so check to see if your local store is connected.

Figure 15-11: Best Buy in action on Twitter.

Best Buy has a Klout Score of 89 (shown in Figure 15-12), and you can find it on Twitter at `https://twitter.com/BestBuy`. You can also ask tech questions by mentioning @Twelpforce or general support questions with @BestBuySupport on Twitter.

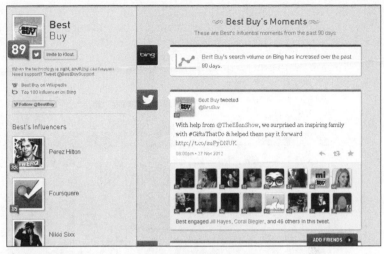

Figure 15-12: Klout Score for Best Buy via Klout.com.

Southwest Airlines

Southwest Airlines (rated on Klout in Figure 15-13) has a reputation for being fun and it certainly maintains that feeling online. With almost 5 million followers between Facebook and Twitter, the folks at Southwest have their work cut out for them. They provide needed information from the airline along with fun contests to engage those of us who aren't traveling at the moment.

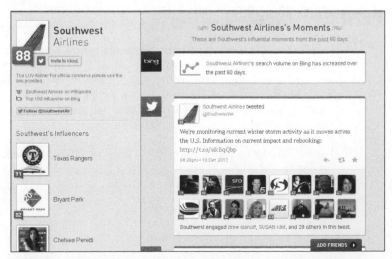

Figure 15-13: Southwest Air isn't connected to Klout, yet it still has a Score.

Southwest Airlines does not have an account with Klout, but based on its public information from Twitter, Klout has assigned it a Score of 88. You can connect with Southwest on Twitter by visiting https://twitter.com/SouthwestAir or Facebook at www.facebook.com/Southwest (shown in Figure 15-14).

Figure 15-14: Facebook Page for Southwest Airlines.

Lands' End

Lands' End is known for its excellent customer service and it's just as friendly online. The folks at Lands' End often share personal photos and ask questions to get their community talking. They have more than 1 million following their Facebook Page, and Twitter (shown in Figure 15-15) is another great way to connect with the team.

Lands' End has a Klout Score of 63 (Figure 15-16). You can find it on Facebook at www.facebook.com/landsend and Twitter by visiting https://twitter.com/LandsEnd.

Figure 15-15: Lands' End connecting with followers via Twitter.

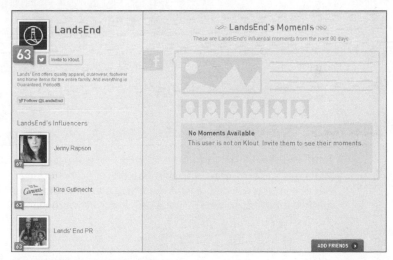

Figure 15-16: Lands' End on Klout.

MOO.com

MOO (shown on Klout in Figure 15-17) is an online printing company that has taken the blogging community by storm. It has a great product and fun packaging along with an easy-to-use website. After you have held a MOO business card, there is no going back. The people at this London-based company know their stuff. What they have done that stands out is they have become part of the community of online content creators. They share relevant and helpful information from business to marketing to social media and cute pets. They are fast and responsive, just like one of your real friends.

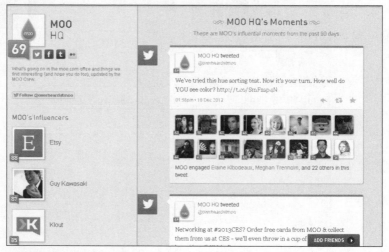

Figure 15-17: MOO.com on Klout.

MOO has a Klout Score of 69 and can be found tweeting at `https://twitter.com/overheardatmoo`. You can also check out its photo tumblr at `http://moohq.tumblr.com` (shown in Figure 15-18).

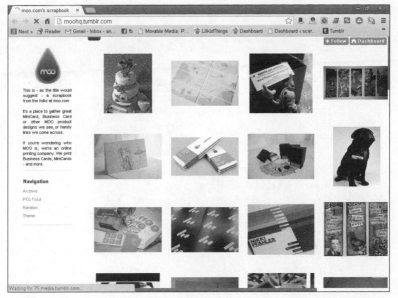

Figure 15-18: Visual feast of MOO creations on its Tumblr page.

TOMS

It's hard not to love a business that gives back. TOMS shoes and eyewear operates on the one-for-one concept. You buy a pair of shoes, and the people at TOMS give a pair of shoes to a child in need. It's as simple as that. They have heart and it shows in their social media accounts (you can see the TOMS Twitter account in Figure 15-19) in the stories they share and the way they promote their followers and fans.

You can be inspired by TOMS on Twitter at `https://twitter.com/TOMS` and on Facebook at `www.facebook.com/toms`. TOMS is not currently a Klout member. Using its public information, however, Klout has assigned it a Score of 82 (shown in Figure 15-20).

Figure 15-19: TOMS on Twitter.

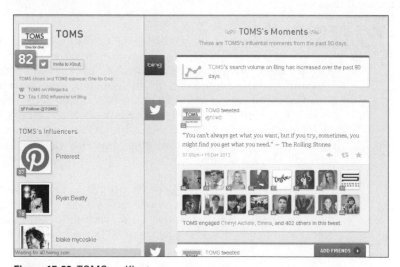

Figure 15-20: TOMS on Klout.

Index

● **F** ●

• L •

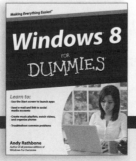

Math & Science

Algebra I For
Dummies, 2nd Edition
978-0-470-55964-2

Anatomy and
Physiology
For Dummies,
2nd Edition
978-0-470-92326-9

Astronomy
For Dummies,
3rd Edition
978-1-118-37697-3

Biology For Dummies,
2nd Edition
978-0-470-59875-7

Chemistry
For Dummies,
2nd Edition
978-1-1180-0730-3

Pre-Algebra Essentials
For Dummies
978-0-470-61838-7

Microsoft Office

Excel 2013
For Dummies
978-1-118-51012-4

Office 2013 All-in-One
For Dummies
978-1-118-51636-2

PowerPoint 2013
For Dummies
978-1-118-50253-2

Word 2013 For Dummies
978-1-118-49123-2

Music

Blues Harmonica
For Dummies
978-1-118-25269-7

Guitar For Dummies,
3rd Edition
978-1-118-11554-1

iPod & iTunes
For Dummies,
10th Edition
978-1-118-50864-0

Programming

Android Application
Development
For Dummies,
2nd Edition
978-1-118-38710-8

iOS 6 Application
Development
For Dummies
978-1-118-50880-0

Java For Dummies,
5th Edition
978-0-470-37173-2

Religion & Inspiration

The Bible
For Dummies
978-0-7645-5296-0

Buddhism For
Dummies, 2nd Edition
978-1-118-02379-2

Catholicism For
Dummies, 2nd Edition
978-1-118-07778-8

Self-Help & Relationships

Bipolar Disorder
For Dummies,
2nd Edition
978-1-118-33882-7

Meditation For
Dummies, 3rd Edition
978-1-118-29144-3

Seniors

Computers For Seniors
For Dummies,
3rd Edition
978-1-118-11553-4

iPad For Seniors
For Dummies,
5th Edition
978-1-118-49708-1

Social Security
For Dummies
978-1-118-20573-0

Smartphones & Tablets

Android Phones
For Dummies
978-1-118-16952-0

Kindle Fire HD
For Dummies
978-1-118-42223-6

NOOK HD
For Dummies,
Portable Edition
978-1-118-39498-4

Surface For Dummies
978-1-118-49634-3

Test Prep

ACT For Dummies,
5th Edition
978-1-118-01259-8

ASVAB For Dummies,
3rd Edition
978-0-470-63760-9

GRE For Dummies,
7th Edition
978-0-470-88921-3

Officer Candidate
Tests, For Dummies
978-0-470-59876-4

Physician's Assistant
Exam For Dummies
978-1-118-11556-5

Series 7 Exam
For Dummies
978-0-470-09932-2

Windows 8

Windows 8
For Dummies
978-1-118-13461-0

Windows 8
For Dummies,
Book + DVD Bundle
978-1-118-27167-4

Windows 8 All-in-One
For Dummies
978-1-118-11920-4

e Available in print and e-book formats.

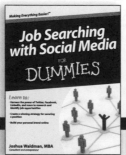

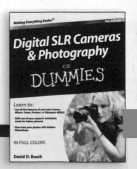

Take Dummies with you everywhere you go!

Whether you're excited about e-books, want more from the web, must have your mobile apps, or swept up in social media, Dummies makes everything easier .